AA

CAR DUFFER'S GUIDE

by Barry Francis

Cartoons by Jo Tapper

2

CONTENTS

Editor: Barry Francis
Designer: Jo Tapper
Technical Consultant: Les Sims
Technical Illustrations: F D Graphics

We gratefully acknowledge the help given by:
Douglas Houston, *Manager of AA Engineering &
Equipment Development*
Peter Denayer, *Senior AA Road Tester*
in the preparation of this book.

Phototypeset by Petty & Sons Ltd, Leeds.
Printed and bound by William Clowes & Sons Ltd, Beccles, Suffolk.
Produced by the Publications Division of the Automobile
Association, Fanum House, Basingstoke, Hants RG21 2EA.

*All the characters in this book are fictitious. Any resemblance to
any persons, living or dead, is entirely coincidental.*

There must be thousands of books about motor cars which all start by assuming that the reader already has some technical knowledge. There are even more 'experts' on motor cars in any 'local' than in all the garages put together, who will glibly air their knowledge over a pint of best bitter (usually at your expense). But neither technical books nor bar-propping know-alls are much good to the real beginner, the 'duffer', who is not ashamed to admit that he, or she, knows as little about motor cars as I know about dressmaking or tuning a fiddle.

I remember the lady journalist who thought it would be a good idea to write a column in her magazine to show what repairs could be made with the things usually found in a lady's handbag. Having studied the most amazing, and intriguing, array of articles she dumped on my desk, I decided that the only advice I could give was to tell her to use her lipstick to write 'HELP!' on the windscreen.

Not long ago my daughter bought her first car. She was almost in tears the next morning when the beast absolutely refused to start. If anything, she was even more infuriated when it started straight away for me. She was puzzled by 'that thing' on the dashboard that I pulled out before turning the ignition key. 'That thing' was

the choke, something she had never needed to use, as her driving instructor had always picked her up from home, by which time the engine of his car was warm.

Similarly, there are those who don't know how to check tyre pressures, how to check the engine oil level or, indeed, carry out any of the other simple, but very important, little jobs that motorists should be able to do for themselves.

My daughter is lucky. If she wants any help or advice it is readily available, but most novices are left to their own devices.

If you look on the motor car as one of life's mysteries, you might like to meet Sid who has been in the garage business all his life and has had more cars than I've had hot dinners. Sid also has the doubtful privilege of having a daughter, a son-in-law and two grandchildren who own a car which is a constant cause of concern to them all. Hardly a day passes without a frantic telephone call for help from the family (reverse charge calls, of course). But Sid is a 'rough diamond' and actually has a soft spot for his family, although he would never admit it, and he dispenses advice to them faster than the local barmaid can pull pints.

He carefully explains how to overcome day-to-day problems but, equally important, he emphasises when it is necessary to call the AA or to have a professional job done at a garage — his, of course.

I hope you will enjoy the adventures of Sid and his family. They are not based on any known persons but, 'if the cap fits . . .'.

A W 'Les' Sims
Manager
AA Technical Services

Thanks, Les. (Nice lad, that. Known him since he was hub high to a pram wheel.) Anyway, wotcher. Yes, I'm Sid. I own this little garage out in the sticks. Actually, I'm London-born and bred. Here, sorry, pull up an oil drum and take the weight off your feet. *Oi! Lionel, put the kettle on, there's a good lad.* Foreman at a place in Dagenham for years I was, until my Else was took nearly twelve year ago.

I felt like a clean break after she passed on, and seeing as the quack told me I shouldn't be breathing in all them carbon dioxide fumes up in the smoke on account of me dicky chest, I decided to move out here with me two boys for a fresh start.

You'd hardly call this place a Palace of Engineering – a pretty ramshackle set-up is nearer the mark, what with the current economic climate restricting investment and so on and so forth. Anyway, it suits us (me and the boys), and we do well enough. My youngest, Lionel, works with me. That's him, or at least his boots, sticking out from under that muck-spreader. He does the greasing and tea-making (both at the same time I sometimes think, judging by the taste of his little perforations) and generally gets under me feet. I always wanted something better for him – I mean,

the opportunities young blokes have got today! It makes me weep to think of him just mucking about here. But no. All he thinks about is bikes and birds and poncing himself up at weekends. Thinks himself another Charlton wossisname – Helston I shouldn't wonder. An image instantly shattered by his grubby fingernails, I might add. 'You want to find yourself a nice girl and settle down my lad,' I tell him. But strewth, who'd have him? Until he pulls himself together and stops all this skylarking about, he'll be a cross I have to bear. But after all's said and done, blood's thicker than wossname, know what I mean?

Now me other boy, Geoffrey, he's different again. He's the bright one of the family. Always reading and studying – I think he'll do well. He shook me the other day by saying he was thinking of taking up brain surgery. 'Blimey,' I says, 'if that's the case, you can do some homework on Lionel.' 'Yeah,' says Geoffrey. 'Turn him into the world's first bionic fitter – only how are you going to come up with a billion dollars?' Actually, I could well do with Geoff on the book-keeping side, only he don't seem interested in business matters. Anyway, we don't

5

see a lot of him what with his lectures and having his head stuck in some weighty tome or another.

Instead, and for my sins, I've got a girl, Janice, who comes in two days a week. She's my girl Friday (and Tuesday). She looks after the paperwork and filing (mainly her nails) in between having her nose stuck in *Reveille*. She's not a lot of cop, but the best I can get around here, and anyway her old man – he's got a farm a couple of miles up the road (that's his muck-spreader over there, by the way) puts quite a bit of business my way. She's a well-built girl

though, blimey, know what I mean? Actually, Lionel fancied her at one time, and asked her to go out with him. She sticks her nose in the air and says, 'I've got bigger fish to fry than you, you scruffy Herbert, thank you very much.' 'Well buzz-off (or words to that effect) and fry 'em,' he says, lobbing a can of hydraulic fluid after her. Never a dull moment here, I tell you!

Which reminds me. The local MP came swanning in here the other morning in his Jag, to settle his petrol account. Perching himself on the edge of Janice's desk, he sits straight on a packet of Stork that she was spreading on her bun. As he leaps up, loud-mouth Lionel pipes up, 'Cor, how's that for a marginal seat?' Fortunately this bloke saw the funny side of it; at least he did after I'd promised to pay for a new pair of pin-stripes. That same afternoon –

no tell a lie, it was the following day – the vicar's lady waltzes in. She keeps herself amused by poking her nose into other people's business. Gets on my wick, she do.
'And what are you trying to do, Sidney?' she enquires in her tea-strainer voice. (I hate it when people say *trying* to do.)
'Bleeding brakes,' I replies, just like that, me hackles rising.
'There's no need for that kind of talk,' she says, all hoity-toity, prodding me ribs with her brolly. How I kept from bursting, I do not know. She got her come-uppance though, by nearly going base-over-wossname over a crankshaft lying on the floor.
'Enjoy the trip?' I shouts, stuffing me head under the wheel arch and chortling to meself.

Oi! Lionel, stop drooling over that Miss Brake-Lining calendar and top these mugs up again. And I'll thank you to save us some of them fast-disappearing custard creams an' all.

Well anyway, that's how things were – swings and roundabouts as you might say. I say *were*, because I've yet to tell you about my daughter Marlene (she's my eldest) and her husband Ron. They moved near here with their two nippers Tracey, who's six, and Tarquin, who's four, on account of their maisonette in Barking being too small for them, what with the kids growing up, not to mention the complaints from their neighbours. Tark was always screaming and hollering round the place and dropping unidentified flying objects on passers-by from the upstairs landing. He was also caught in a compromising situation with the little girl from next door, but the least said about that the better. I put me big foot in it by saying that the kids needed a decent garden to play in and a proper house to expand in, and why not move nearer here? I didn't mean on the flaming doorstep though – much as I love them. Anyway, next thing I know they've moved in about a mile away. I mean, I wouldn't have minded so much if it hadn't been for their new car. Huh! I say 'new' but I really mean new to them. They bought it about a week or two after they'd settled in, and they came bowling round here in it as pleased as Punch, asking us what we thought of it. Trying to keep a straight face I says, 'Blimey, where d'you get this then, Sotheby's? I'll say one thing for it, Ron, it's got a generous coating of oxide of iron.'

'Oh, is that good?' asks Marle hopefully.

'No, it's rust,' says Lionel with a leer.

'Oh, I'm not worried by a bit of rust,' says Ron defensively.

'The friend of a friend I got it from said it was a very good model – built to last.'

So was the *Titanic,* I thought. Well you should have seen it.

'OK, it's not perfect,' he went on. 'But it does all we want.'

'Ah well, *shackern ar song goo*', says Geoffrey.

'Yeah, and to each his own, an' all,' I said.

'Anyway,' chips in Marlene with a pout. 'You'll help us out with any snags that might crop up, won't you Dad?'

'Innit marvellous?' I says. 'You come round here in something what looks like it should of been left out for the dustmen, telling me it ain't perfect, and expecting me to keep it going as though I got nothing else to do; what a liberty! Don't consult me before you buy it, do you? Don't consider what it does for the garage's reputation? What are people going to think seeing Sid Trimble's daughter chugging about in this apology for a motor? And I suppose you've gone and taxed it for a whole year an' all.' By now I'd worked meself up into a state and was starting to puff and wheeze.

'Cool it, Dad,' says Lionel.

'Yeah,' adds Geoffrey. 'Remember what the doc said about getting over-excited.'

'All right, all right,' I says, stomping off for one of me tablets. When I got back they'd gone.

'Pushed off, have they?' I says casually.

'Yeah,' says Lionel with a smirk. 'Slammed off in a hell of a temper. What shall I do with this door handle?'

'Stick it in that cardboard box what we'll label 'Marlene's Droppings' – it's only the first of many, or I'm a monkey's wossname,' I says.

After a sit down and a mug of Lionel's sump oil, I began to feel guilty about losing me rag like that. Wasn't I young and impetuous meself once? And blimey, they're me own kith and kin after all's said and done. So I rang them up to apologise didn't I? 'Bring it round love,' I says to Marlene who'd cooled off herself by then. 'I'll take a look at it.'

'Thanks, Dad,' she said. 'Tell the truth I wasn't too happy when I saw what Ron had gone and bought. But he was so chuffed, I didn't like to spoil things for him. You know what he's like!'

''Nuf said Marle,' I says. 'But I can't guarantee to make a silk purse out of a sow's wossname. I'll do me best though, and if you get into any bother just give us a buzz – any time.'

'You're a sweetie, Dad,' she says. 'I'll give you an orange at Christmas. 'Bye for now.'

'Course I'd signed me own death warrant then, hadn't I? Blimey, that car (for want of a better word) – 'Snowdrop' it was called, would you believe? – was round here so often I swear it knew its own way. When it wasn't sitting in here, Marlene or Ron was on the hot line with some trouble or other. The tales I could tell you; in fact if you haven't got to rush off, I will. Take last November for instance, it started off a beautiful day; then the phone rang . . .

HI DAD, IT'S ME. LISTEN, THE DOOR LOCKS ARE FROZEN UP AND I CAN'T GET IN. WHAT CAN I DO? I SHOULD HAVE HAD THE KIDS AT SCHOOL TEN MINUTES AGO!
WELL, WHERE'S THAT SPECIAL DOOR LOCK DE-ICER AEROSOL I GAVE YOU? IN THE GLOVE-BOX I SUPPOSE. TRY HEATING THE KEY WITH A LIGHTER OR A MATCH BEFORE YOU PUSH IT IN THE KEYHOLE. DON'T HOLD THE FLAME TO THE LOCK ITSELF OR YOU'LL DAMAGE THE PAINT. AND DON'T USE A FLAME ON THE PETROL CAP LOCK. IF THAT DON'T WORK, TRY HOLDING A CLOTH SOAKED IN VERY HOT WATER TO THE KEYHOLE AREA.
A HAIR DRYER WOULD DO THE TRICK, ONLY YOU'LL NEED A FLIPPIN' LONG EXTENSION LEAD.

JUST LATELY THERE'S BEEN SOME OMINOUS-LOOKING DRIPS COMING FROM THE EXHAUST PIPE WHEN I'VE STARTED THE ENGINE FROM COLD. IT LOOKS LIKE WATER; DOES IT MEAN THERE'S A LEAK IN THE ENGINE OR SOMETHING?

NO, DON'T PANIC, RON. NOW THE COLDER WEATHER'S SET IN, THE HOT EXHAUST IS CONDENSING INTO WATER AND THAT'S WHAT'S DRIPPING FROM THE TAILPIPE. FORGET IT, IT'S NORMAL. YOU PROBABLY HAVEN'T NOTICED IT BEFORE, THAT'S ALL.

Business, Pleasure and Holiday Leisure...

HOTELS AND RESTAURANTS IN BRITAIN
All impartially inspected, this guide lists 5,000 AA approved places to stay or wine and dine in comfort.

999 PLACES TO EAT OUT FOR AROUND £5
Dining out on a budget. From the exotic to the plain at a price everyone can afford.

STATELY HOMES, MUSEUMS, CASTLES AND GARDENS IN BRITAIN
Over 2,000 places to visit on days out. Historic houses, zoos, wildlife parks, monuments and more.

CAMPING AND CARAVANNING IN BRITAIN
For veterans and beginners alike. Features around 900 sites checked for quality and maintenance of facilities offered.

SELF-CATERING IN BRITAIN
A vast choice for the independent holidaymaker — flats, chalets, cottages and houses.

GUESTHOUSES, FARMHOUSES AND INNS IN BRITAIN
Thousands of inexpensive places with comfortable accommodation, good food and friendly faces.

 **AA Publications**

Available from AA shops and major booksellers.

1

AS IF THIS COLD, DAMP WEATHER WASN'T BAD ENOUGH, SNOWDROP JUST WON'T START. ALTHOUGH THE ENGINE SPINS OVER QUITE WELL (I'VE BEEN CAREFUL NOT TO CANE THE BATTERY, LIKE YOU ALWAYS SAY) IT SOUNDS AND FEELS SORT OF LIFELESS, D'YOU KNOW WHAT I MEAN? THERE'S QUITE A SMELL OF PETROL, THOUGH.

I RECKON IT'S CONDENSATION WHAT'S CAUSING IT — YOU'VE GOT DAMP ELECTRICS, I BET. LIFT THE BONNET AND WIPE THE DISTRIBUTOR CAP, HT LEADS, COIL AND PLUG TOPS WITH A CLOTH OR TISSUES TO GET THE WORST OF THE MOISTURE OFF. THEN GET RON'S WATER REPELLING AEROSOL SPRAY AND SQUIRT IT LIGHTLY OVER ALL THE BITS I'VE JUST MENTIONED. THAT SHOULD DO THE TRICK.

CONTINUED:—

2 BUT HOLD IT, MARLE. IF YOU'VE BEEN CHURNING AWAY ON THE STARTER YOU COULD HAVE FLOODED THE ENGINE, AND IT STILL MIGHT NOT START 'COS IT'S OVER-RICH. SO, PUSH THE CHOKE RIGHT IN, PRESS THE ACCELERATOR SLOWLY TO THE FLOOR AND HOLD IT THERE, THEN WORK THE STARTER — FOR QUITE A FEW SECONDS IF NECESSARY. WITH A BIT OF LUCK THE ENGINE SHOULD BURST INTO LIFE. IT MIGHT NEED A BIT OF CHOKE THEN TO KEEP IT RUNNING.

THANKS, DAD.
THIS ALWAYS HAPPENS
WHEN I'M IN A RUSH
AH WELL,
LET US SPRAY!

HAVE YOU GOT A MINUTE, DAD? I'VE BEEN GIVING THE ENGINE COMPARTMENT THE ONCE-OVER AND I'VE NOTICED THAT THE BATTERY'S IN A BIT OF A MESS. THERE'S A SORT OF WHITE, WOOLLY FUNGUS GROWING ROUND THE TERMINALS. AND DO YOU THINK I OUGHT TO CHECK THE STRENGTH OF THE WHATSIT — ELECTROLYTE — WHILE I'M AT IT? YOU KNOW, SEE WHAT THE STATE OF THE CHARGE IS.

WHAT YOU CALL 'WOOLLY FUNGUS' RON, IS CORROSION. TO GET IT OFF YOU'LL HAVE TO REMOVE THE TERMINALS. THEN CLEAN OFF THE CORROSION (WARM WATER WILL SHIFT IT QUICKLY), AND SHINE UP THE TERMINAL POSTS WITH A BIT OF EMERY CLOTH OR WIRE WOOL. NEXT, SMEAR THE POSTS LIGHTLY WITH VASELINE. FINALLY, REFIT THE TERMINALS FIRMLY. WHILE YOU'RE AT IT, CHECK THAT THE OTHER END OF THE EARTH WIRE IS CONNECTED GOOD AND TIGHT TO THE BODY OR ENGINE AND THAT THE OLD RUST BUG ISN'T 'AVING A GO THERE TOO.

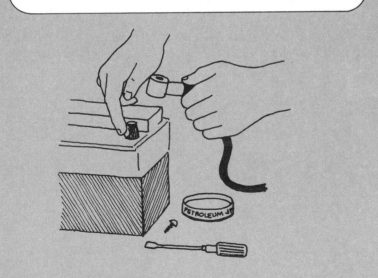

CONTINUED:—

2

OK. NOW WHAT ABOUT THE ELECTROLYTE? I'VE BORROWED A HYDROMETER FROM ONE OF ME MATES, BUT I DON'T KNOW WHAT TO DO WITH IT.

I COULD TELL YOU WHAT TO DO WITH IT, RON! — BUT INSTEAD YOU'D BETTER REMOVE THE FILLER CAPS AND DIP THE THIN END OF THE HYDROMETER INTO EACH CELL IN TURN, (HAVING MADE SURE THAT THE CELLS ARE TOPPED UP WITH DISTILLED WATER FIRST). SQUEEZE THE BULB AND SUCK IN ENOUGH ELECTROLYTE TO RAISE THE FLOAT. THEN TAKE THE READING WHERE THE FLOAT BREAKS THE SURFACE. ALWAYS RETURN THE ELECTROLYTE TO THE CELL IT CAME FROM. FOR A FULLY CHARGED BATTERY, THE READING SHOULD BE BETWEEN 1.270 AND 1.290. IF IT IS BELOW 1.250 THE BATTERY NEEDS CHARGING.

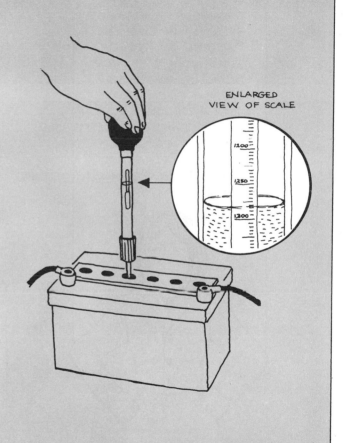

ENLARGED VIEW OF SCALE

DAD, HELP! THERE WAS A 'DONK' WHEN I TRIED TO START SNOWDROP JUST NOW, AND THEN NOTHING HAPPENED — ONLY A CLICK FROM UNDER THE BONNET EVERY TIME I TURNED THE KEY. I'M LIVID — I'LL HAVE TO GO TO BINGO BY BUS, UNLESS THERE'S ANYTHING I CAN DO.

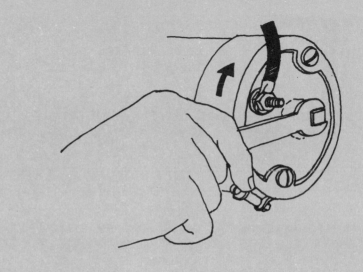

THE STARTER MOTOR PINION'S PROBABLY STUCK — COULD BE IT'S MUCKY OR THE TEETH ARE WORN. TRY TO FREE IT WITH A SPANNER BY TURNING THE SQUARE END STICKING OUT OF THE FRONT OF THE MOTOR. PULL THE METAL CAP OFF FIRST THOUGH, IF IT'S GOT ONE. WORK THE SPANNER UP AND DOWN AND TURN IT CLOCKWISE TO WIND THE PINION OUT.

CONTINUED:-

2 IF THAT DON'T WORK, PUT THE CAR INTO TOP GEAR, TAKE THE HANDBRAKE OFF AND THEN ROCK THE CAR TO AND FRO. YOU MIGHT NEED SOME HELP HERE. DON'T GO TOO VIOLENT THOUGH, OR YOU'LL BEND SOMETHING.

IF IT WON'T FREE, YOU'VE HAD IT. THE MOTOR WILL HAVE TO COME OFF. I'D BETTER HAVE IT OFF TO CLEAN AND INSPECT IT ANYWAY, OTHERWISE IT'S LIKELY TO STICK AGAIN.

PETROL

OH, YOU'RE SMASHING, DAD! THERE'S A COUPLE OF BROWN ALES IN IT FOR YOU. 'BYE.

1

HEY DAD, I'VE BEEN FIDDLING ABOUT FOR AGES TRYING TO GET THE WINDSCREEN WASHERS TO WORK PROPERLY. THEY'VE BEEN PLAYING UP LATELY AND I MUST HAVE THEM RIGHT FOR ME M O T TEST. ANYWAY, I HATE DRIVING WITH A MUCKY SCREEN, ESPECIALLY AT NIGHT.

STREWTH RON! I TOLD YOU WHAT THE TROUBLE WAS DAYS AGO. THE WASHER RESERVOIR'S FULL OF SLIME AND THE LITTLE FILTER ON THE END OF THE PLASTIC TUBE IS BLOCKED. PULL IT OFF AND FLUSH IT CLEAN WITH WATER. ALSO CLEAN OUT THE RESERVOIR THOROUGHLY — YOU'VE BEEN NEGLECTING IT. BLOW THROUGH THE PIPES, AND IF THE JETS ARE BLOCKED, PRICK THEM OUT WITH A PIN. TOP UP WITH CLEAN WATER AND ADD A SACHET OF SCREENWASH FLUID — THE SORT THAT'S GOT AN ANTI-FREEZE IN IT AN' ALL.

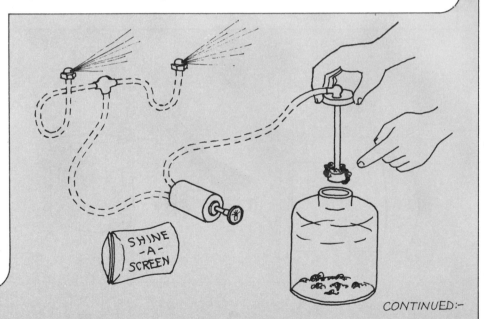

SHINE -A- SCREEN

CONTINUED:-

2

ACTUALLY THOUGH, THAT ISN'T
WAS ON ABOUT.
I HAVE TO KEEP PUMPING THE KNOB
BEFORE ANY WATER SQUIRTS OUT,
AFTER THE CAR'S BEEN STANDING.

AH. WELL, YOUR ONE-WAY VALVE'S
UP THE SWANEE.
THE WATER ISN'T BEING HELD IN
THE TUBES, IT'S DRAINING BACK
INTO THE RESERVOIR. YOU NEED A
NEW VALVE, IT'S EASY TO FIT.
PULL OFF THE OLD ONE AND PUSH
ON A REPLACEMENT. SOME VALVES
ARE BUILT INTO THE PICK-UP END
(WHERE THE FILTER IS), SOME ARE
IN THE SUPPLY PIPE — IT ALL
DEPENDS. TAKE THE OLD ONE TO
THE ACCESSORY SHOP AS A
PATTERN IF YOU'RE GOING TO
DO IT YOURSELF — PLEASE!

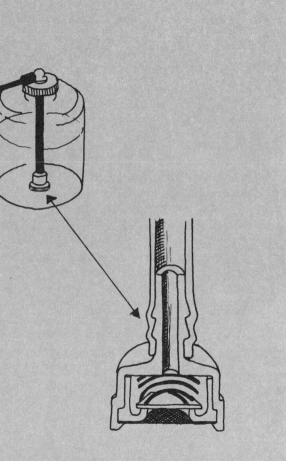

1

PHEW! I'VE JUST HAD A BIT OF A SHOCK! A STONE'S SMASHED THE WINDSCREEN, BUT I MANAGED TO STOP ALL RIGHT. NOW I'M STUCK IN THIS LAY-BY — THERE'S GLASS EVERYWHERE IN THE CAR. WHAT'S THE BEST THING TO DO, DAD?

YEAH, WELL. YOU'D BEST GET YOURSELF ORGANISED. YOU'VE GOT ONE OF THEM EMERGENCY WINDSCREENS IN THE BOOT, HAVEN'T YOU? START BY LAYING A PIECE OF CLOTH OR NEWSPAPER ON THE BONNET, AND COVER THE DEMISTER VENTS TOO, YOU DON'T WANT BITS OF GLASS DROPPING INTO THE HEATER. THEN SPREAD MORE PAPER OR WHAT-HAVE-YOU ON THE FLOOR, BECAUSE MOST OF THE GLASS IS GOING TO FALL INTO THE CAR NOW CAREFULLY EASE THE BROKEN GLASS OUT OF THE SURROUND WITHOUT CUTTING YOURSELF. IT'S NOT SAFE TO DRIVE ALONG PEERING THROUGH A LITTLE HOLE.

CONTINUED :-

2

WHEN YOU'VE GOT ALL THE GLASS OUT, WRAP IT UP AND GET RID OF IT PROPERLY. DON'T JUST DUMP IT ANYWHERE — TAKE IT HOME WITH YOU IF NECESSARY. NOW FIT THE EMERGENCY WINDSCREEN — FULL INSTRUCTIONS ARE ON THE BOX. BEFORE YOU DRIVE OFF, CLEAN UP THE INTERIOR AS BEST YOU CAN. OH, AND DON'T LOSE YOUR TAX DISC!

EMERGENCY WINDSCREEN

AA

HOW FAST CAN I DRIVE WITH THE EMERGENCY SCREEN, AND CAN I USE THE WIPERS IF IT RAINS?

WELL, IF YOU WIND UP ALL THE WINDOWS (AS YOU SHOULD) IT'LL BE O K TO 40 OR 50 M P H. THE WIPERS SHOULD WORK QUITE WELL AN' ALL. THESE SCREENS VARY A BIT FROM MAKE TO MAKE, BUT THE INSTRUCTIONS WILL GIVE YOU ALL THE GEN.

CONTINUED :—

3

ONCE I GET THE NEW WINDSCREEN, I WANT TO LOOK AFTER IT. THE OLD ONE WAS A BIT MARKED. REMEMBER HOW RON WENT AND SCRATCHED IT WHEN HE WAS SCRAPING OFF THAT ICE LAST WINTER?

DO I NOT? THE DAFT TWIT! FANCY USING A HACKSAW BLADE I TOLD HIM TO USE A PROPER DE-ICER SPRAY AND A PLASTIC OR WOODEN SCRAPER. ACTUALLY, A METHS-SOAKED CLOTH AND A CREDIT CARD, OR SOMETHING SIMILAR, WORK QUITE WELL IN AN EMERGENCY. A HANDY TOOL, THOUGH, IS ONE OF THEM COMBINED SPONGE/ RUBBER SCRAPER WOSSNAMES. IT CLEANS THE SCREEN AND WINDOWS QUICKLY, ONCE THE AEROSOL HAS TURNED THE ICE TO SLUSH.

ANOTHER THING — DON'T LET THE WIPERS GRIND AWAY ON A DRY WINDSCREEN. IT'S A SURE WAY TO RUIN THE BLADES, MARK THE GLASS, OR DAMAGE THE WIPER MOTOR.

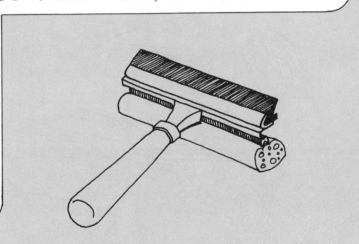

PERHAPS THIS IS A GOOD POINT FOR ME TO MENTION WHAT I KEEP TRYING TO DRUM INTO MARLENE AND RON. DON'T FORGET YOUR ESSENTIAL WEEKLY CHECKS ON THE CAR.

* TYRE PRESSURES – INCLUDING SPARE
* ENGINE OIL LEVEL
* WATER LEVEL IN RADIATOR
* TOP UP BATTERY IF NECESSARY
* CHECK THAT ALL YOUR LIGHTS WORK

REMEMBER TOO, THAT SKIMPING ON SERVICING IS DAFT. THE NUMBER OF MOTORS I SEE WHOSE BONNETS HAVEN'T BEEN LIFTED FOR WHAT LOOKS LIKE YEARS ON END IS DIABOLICAL. REGULAR MAINTENANCE NOT ONLY PREVENTS A LOT OF AGGRO, IT ALSO SAVES YOU MONEY IN THE LONG RUN.

1 DAD, WE'RE IN DEAD LUMBER AGAIN. WE'RE ON OUR WAY BACK FROM THE SUPERMARKET AND THE WIPERS HAVE PACKED UP. THEY STOPPED SUDDENLY — JUST LIKE THAT! THIS DRIZZLE LOOKS LIKE IT'S SET IN FOR THE DAY. IS THERE ANYTHING I CAN DO? THERE'S A FUNNY SMELL FROM SOMEWHERE, TOO.

NO, YOU CAN'T REALLY DO NOTHING. IN THE OLD DAYS I USED TO CUT A SPUD IN HALF AND RUB IT OVER THE WINDSCREEN TO BREAK UP THE RAINDROPS. THAT GAVE REASONABLE VISION TO GET HOME WITH. TROUBLE IS NOW, THAT IT'S ILLEGAL TO DRIVE WITH FAULTY WIPERS. I'LL HAVE TO COME AND PICK YOU UP IN THE TRUCK, I SUPPOSE, BUT BEFORE I TURN OUT, MAKE SURE IT AIN'T SIMPLY AN OLD FUSE THAT'S BLOWN, CAUSING THE FAILURE. THIS GOES FOR MOST OF THE ELECTRICAL PARTS THAT PACK UP — CHECK THE FUSES FIRST. I GIVE MARLE A SET OF SPARES AND TOLD HER TO KEEP 'EM IN THE GLOVEBOX. MAKE SURE THE NEW ONE IS THE SAME AMPERAGE AS THE OLD ONE, IF THAT IS THE TROUBLE.

1 OOH, CRIKEY! SNOWDROP'S DRIVING POSITION IS GIVING ME ACHES AND PAINS. I SIT TOO LOW AND THE CUSHION IS TOO FLAT — I DON'T GET ANY THIGH SUPPORT. I'M FED UP WITH CRANING MY NECK TO SEE OUT. IS THERE ANY ALTERNATIVE TO SITTING ON A CUSHION?

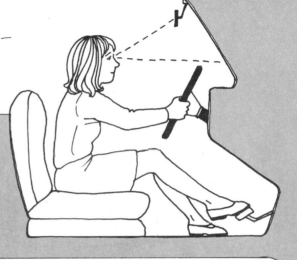

NIL CARBORUNDUM, MY LOVE. BRING HER ROUND AND I'LL SEE WHAT I CAN DO, AFTER I'VE FINISHED ME SANDWICHES.

IF THE SEAT RUNNERS ARE BOLTED TO THE FLOOR, I CAN PROBABLY RAISE AND TILT THE SEAT WITH BIG WASHERS, OR TAPERED PIECES OF WOOD.

ONLY IT'S NOT A JOB TO BE BOTCHED, SO DON'T LET RON START MESSING ABOUT. I'LL DO THE JOB PROPERLY WITH LONGER BOLTS, AND MAKE SURE THAT THE SEAT IS REALLY FIRMLY MOUNTED. A BADLY FIXED SEAT CAN BE DANGEROUS, BUT THEN SO CAN NOT SEEING OUT PROPERLY THROUGH THE WINDSCREEN.

CONTINUED :—

2

MMM, THAT SOUNDS HOPEFUL, BUT THE PEDALS ARE TOO HIGH FOR MY DAINTY FEET. IS THERE ANYTHING YOU CAN THINK OF, SHORT OF OVERSIZE WELLIES?

WELL, YOU CAN'T DRIVE IN <u>THEM</u>. NO, I CAN FIX A WOODEN BLOCK WITH CHAMFERED EDGES FIRMLY UNDER THE CARPET IN FRONT OF THE PEDALS. EASY! AND BY THE WAY, THERE ARE ALL SORTS OF THINGS THEY SELL IN ACCESSORY SHOPS TO ALTER YOUR DRIVING POSITION : GEAR LEVER EXTENSIONS, DISHED STEERING WHEELS, STEERING COLUMN ADJUSTERS, PEDAL PADS, SHAPED SEAT BACKRESTS — THINGS LIKE THAT. IT'S WORTH HAVING A BROWSE NEXT TIME YOU'RE IN TOWN.

BUT HOW ARE ALL THESE MODS GOING TO SUIT RON?

THAT <u>IS</u> A PROBLEM, OF COURSE, BUT I CAN'T PLEASE EVERYONE, CAN I?

CONTINUED:—

3

AND MARLE, HAVE YOU DONE ANYTHING ABOUT THAT WORN CARPET I TOLD YOU ABOUT? YOU'LL CATCH YOUR HEELS IN IT, AND IT WILL GET CAUGHT UP ROUND THE PEDALS AND STOP THEM FROM MOVING PROPERLY. YOUR PEDAL RUBBERS NEED REPLACING TOO, THEY'RE ALL SMOOTH AND SHINY. IF YOUR FEET SLIP OFF 'EM, IT COULD BE NASTY!

YES, I HAVE. RON'S TIDIED THE CARPET UP AND FITTED A RUBBER FLOOR MAT, AND HE'S ALSO FITTED TWO NEW PEDAL RUBBERS MUCH GRIPPIER THEY ARE, SPECIALLY WHEN MY SHOES ARE WET.

DAD, THERE'S A PECULIAR SPLASHING NOISE COMING FROM THE DOORS WHEN THE CAR IS MOVING, ESPECIALLY WHEN I BRAKE OR ACCELERATE. IT SOUNDS LIKE WATER!

IT PROBABLY IS, LOVE. IT SOUNDS AS THOUGH YOUR DOOR DRAIN HOLES ARE BLOCKED, AND THE DOORS ARE FILLING UP WITH RAIN WATER. CLEAR 'EM OUT WITH A LENGTH OF STIFF WIRE, AND LET THE WATER OUT. KEEP 'EM CLEAR TOO, OTHERWISE THE BOTTOM OF THE DOORS WILL ROT AWAY. DOUBLE QUICK.

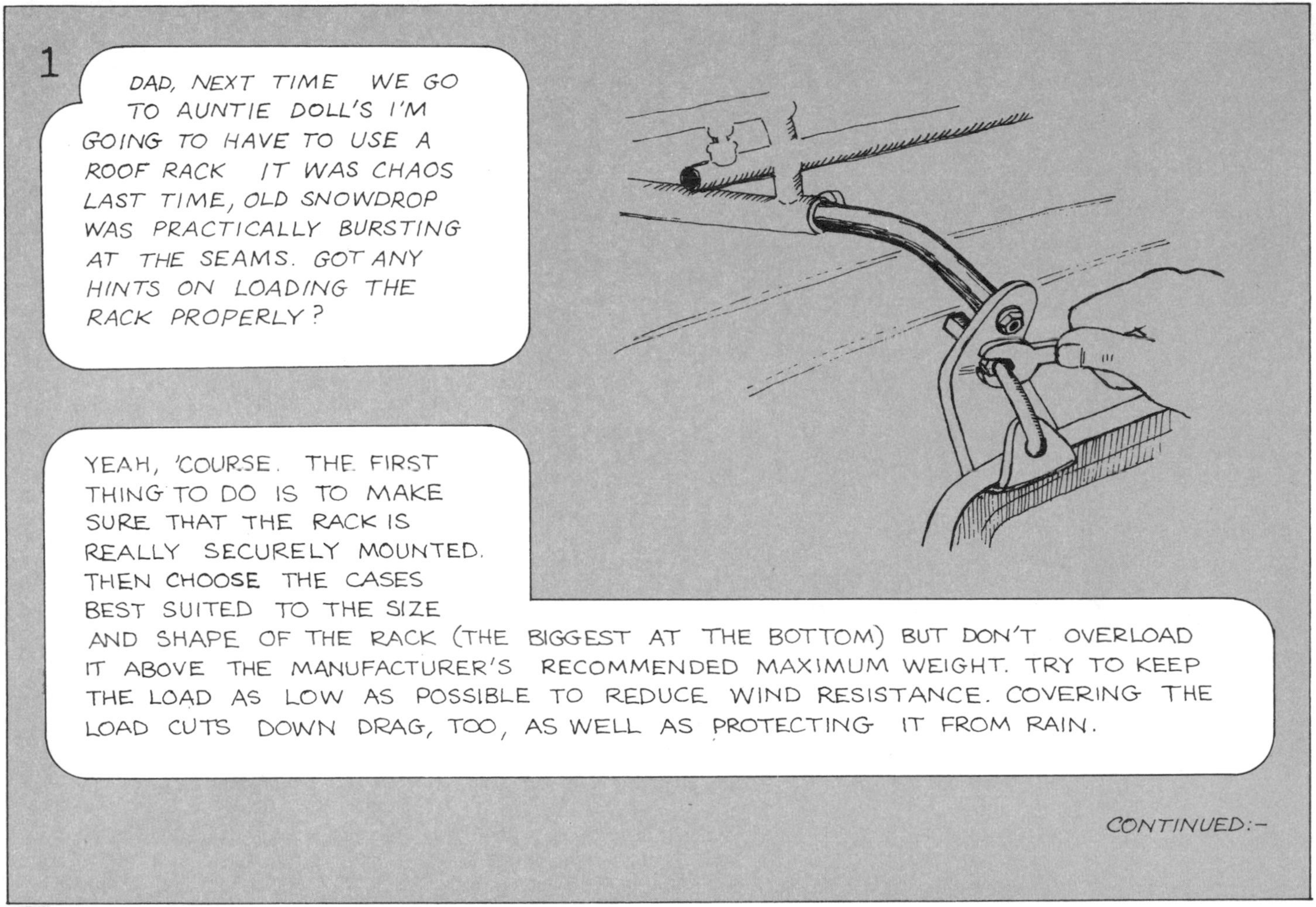

1

DAD, NEXT TIME WE GO TO AUNTIE DOLL'S I'M GOING TO HAVE TO USE A ROOF RACK. IT WAS CHAOS LAST TIME, OLD SNOWDROP WAS PRACTICALLY BURSTING AT THE SEAMS. GOT ANY HINTS ON LOADING THE RACK PROPERLY?

YEAH, 'COURSE. THE FIRST THING TO DO IS TO MAKE SURE THAT THE RACK IS REALLY SECURELY MOUNTED. THEN CHOOSE THE CASES BEST SUITED TO THE SIZE AND SHAPE OF THE RACK (THE BIGGEST AT THE BOTTOM) BUT DON'T OVERLOAD IT ABOVE THE MANUFACTURER'S RECOMMENDED MAXIMUM WEIGHT. TRY TO KEEP THE LOAD AS LOW AS POSSIBLE TO REDUCE WIND RESISTANCE. COVERING THE LOAD CUTS DOWN DRAG, TOO, AS WELL AS PROTECTING IT FROM RAIN.

CONTINUED:-

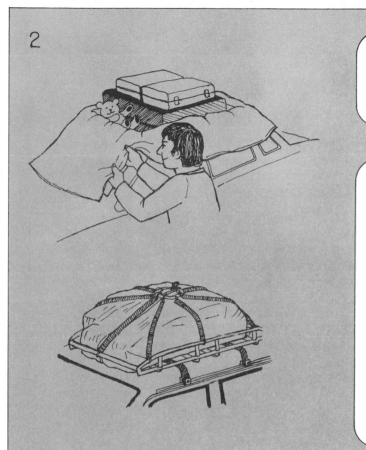

WHAT'S THE BEST WAY TO COVER THE CASES THEN? I'VE GOT A BIG SHEET OF POLYTHENE. I SUPPOSE I COULD USE THAT, COULDN'T I?

WELL YOU CAN, BUT IT WILL PROBABLY FLAP ABOUT AND BE IN TATTERS IN A FEW MILES. BEST USE A DECENT SHEET OF PVC OR CANVAS, PUTTING THE LUGGAGE ON IT, THEN FOLDING IT BACK OVER TO STOP THE WIND GETTING UNDER NEATH. TIE IT DOWN TIGHT WITH ROPE OR STRONG ELASTICS AND CHECK THAT BOTH THE RACK AND ITS LOAD ARE STILL SECURE AFTER YOU'VE DRIVEN TEN MILES OR SO, WHEN THINGS HAVE SETTLED DOWN.
TAKE THE RACK OFF WHEN YOU'VE DONE WITH IT, OTHERWISE YOU'LL GET WIND HUM AND YOUR PETROL CONSUMPTION WILL SUFFER.

HEY DAD. CAN YOU COME ROUND AND LISTEN TO THIS? THERE'S A FUNNY HIGH-PITCHED WARBLING FROM THE FRONT OF THE ENGINE. IT'S QUITE LOUD, SPECIALLY WHEN THE ENGINE'S TICKING OVER. I'M NOT REALLY HAPPY ABOUT DRIVING A CAR WITH THE TWITTERS.

OH, I THINK IT'LL BE O K TO DRIVE, RON. IT'S THE WATER-PUMP SEAL THAT'S DRY AND SQUEALING. WORN PUMP BEARINGS USUALLY MAKE A LOUD RUMBLING NOISE. BUT JUST CHECK THAT THE BEARINGS ARE ALL RIGHT. TAKE HOLD OF OPPOSITE BLADES OF THE COOLING FAN AND TRY TO WAGGLE THEM BACKWARDS AND FORWARDS. THERE SHOULDN'T BE ANY FREE MOVEMENT OR KNOCKING NOISES.
YOU CAN CURE THE SQUEAL BY BUYING A CAN OF WATER-PUMP LUBRICANT AND POURING IT INTO THE RADIATOR. REMEMBER WHAT I SAID ABOUT NOT SCALDING YOURSELF THOUGH, IF THE WATER'S HOT.

Given your car insurance its
cost/cover checkup yet?

It's a free **AA** service

Don't leave it too late. There's a simple way to make certain you've got the right motor insurance cover for your needs, at the best price going. Just check your existing policy against an AA quotation. Do it now — by filling in the checklist overleaf. There can be other benefits in an AA policy. Payments by easy instalments for example. If you are over 50 or your car is over 6 years old, we could get you a useful discount. Or save up to 20% if only you and your wife drive the car. With other big discounts for certain occupations. How much of this value are you missing at present? Check and see.

Answer the questions overleaf — clear block capitals please. Then tear out the complete page and post it in an unstamped envelope addressed to: AA Insurance Services Limited, FREEPOST, Newcastle upon Tyne NE99 2RP.

just fill in the checklist overleaf

FILL IN FOR YOUR FREE AA CAR INSURANCE QUOTATION — POSTING DETAILS ON REVERSE

About yourself

Please use BLOCK CAPITALS

initials   surname

Mr / Mrs/Miss

Address

Post Code

Daytime Telephone No.

Membership No. (or write non-member)

Occupation

Employer's business

When would you like cover to commence?

On that date (a) How old will you be?

(b) How long will you have been resident in the UK?   yrs

(c) How long will you have held a full UK driving licence?   yrs

(d) How many years No Claim Discount will you have earned in your own right?   yrs

Name of your present Insurance Company

day month year

FOR OFFICE USE ONLY

About your car

Make and model of car including details of modifications

Engine cc .... Year of manufacture 19 ......   Value £

When do you use your car?

*Please delete the word that does not apply
In addition to private use, will the car be used for:

(a) Driving to work on three or more days a week?   YES/NO*

If yes, name city, town or suburb where you work.
Is your place of work more than 10 miles from your home?   YES/NO*

(b) Business use by yourself only?   YES/NO*

(c) Business use by any other person?   YES/NO*

(d) Commercial travelling?   YES/NO*

(e) What is your estimated annual mileage? .... miles

Have you or any other person who will drive this car

(a) Been convicted of any driving offence other than parking?   YES/NO*

(b) Been involved in any accident in the last five years?   YES/NO*

(c) Suffer from any physical disability or infirmity
e.g. heart disease etc?   YES/NO*

If you have answered yes to 'a','b' or 'c' please give details on separate sheet.
Please indicate (✓) who will drive the vehicle:

(a) Yourself only

(b) Yourself and wife/husband only

(c) Yourself and one named driver only

(d) Any licensed driver

In the case of (b) and (c) please give details of other driver
or in the case of (d) details of youngest known driver. Age

Length full UK Driving Licence held?

What cover do you want?

Please tick the type of cover you require:

Comprehensive [ ]   Third Party Fire & Theft [ ]   Third Party Only [ ]

Do you wish to reduce the premium by bearing up to £25,
£35 or £50 of the cost of any damage to your car?   YES/NO*
If yes, please write your choice here   £

313

Registered Office: Fanum House Basingstoke Hants RG21 2EA Regd No. 912191 England

DAD, I'VE BEEN MEANING TO ASK YOU ABOUT THE CHATTERING NOISE FROM SNOWDROP'S GEARBOX — LEAST, I THINK IT'S FROM THE BOX. IT ONLY HAPPENS IN NEUTRAL AND DISAPPEARS WHEN I PUSH THE CLUTCH OUT, BUT IT'S BEEN GOING ON FOR SOME TIME NOW. DO YOU THINK IT'S SERIOUS AND I SHOULD DO SOMETHING ABOUT IT?

I'LL HAVE TO LISTEN TO IT NEXT TIME YOU'RE IN MARLE, BUT I RECKON IT'S ONLY THE IDLER GEARS RATTLING A BIT — IT'S QUITE COMMON ON THAT MODEL. IF IT'S NOT REALLY BAD I SHOULD LEAVE WELL ALONE — IT WON'T DO ANY HARM.
IT STOPS WHEN YOU PUSH THE CLUTCH OUT 'COS NOTHING IN THE GEARBOX IS TURNING THEN, ALL THE GEARS ARE STATIONARY.

1

HI DAD. NO, DON'T PANIC, ITS NOT ABOUT SNOWDROP THIS TIME, BELIEVE IT OR NOT. IT'S ABOUT MY GUV'NOR'S CAR. IT'S GOT FRONT DISC BRAKES, SEE AND HE'S COMPLAINING ABOUT THEM SQUEALING WHEN HE PUTS THEM ON. IT'S 'FRIGHTFULLY IRRITATING' ACCORDING TO HIM. I SAID I'D HAVE A WORD WITH YOU ABOUT THEM.

YEAH, WELL IT DOES GET ON YOUR WICK. IT'S NOT ALWAYS EASY TO CURE, EITHER. SOMETIMES IT'S CAUSED BY BRAKE PAD DUST BUILDING UP, OR IT COULD BE THAT THE PADS ARE GLAZED — YOU KNOW, THEIR SURFACE IS ALL SORT OF HARD AND GLASSY. TELL HIM TO HAVE 'EM LOOKED AT A GENERAL CLEAN UP AND NEW SET OF PADS WILL PROBABLY BE THE ANSWER — AT LEAST FOR A TIME.

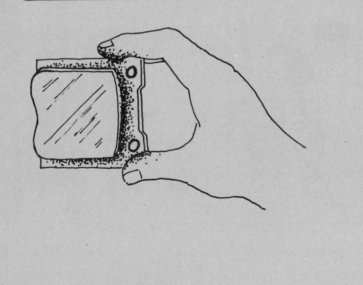

CONTINUED:-

2

THE OTHER THING WAS ABOUT HOW DIRTY HIS FRONT WHEELS GET. WHEN IT COMES ROUND TO THE CAR'S WEEKLY WASH, THEY'RE COVERED IN BLACK, SOOTY-LOOKING POWDER.

MMM! THAT'S DUST FROM THE BRAKE PADS AGAIN. IT GETS BLOWN OUT THROUGH THE HOLES IN THE WHEELS AS THE CAR IS MOVING, AND LOOKS MESSY. NOTHING MUCH HE CAN DO ABOUT IT. HE'LL JUST HAVE TO KEEP WASHING IT OFF REGULARLY. WITH PLENTY OF SOAPY WATER, OR A BRUSHING WITH PARAFFIN WILL SHIFT IT.
IT'S JUST ONE OF THEM THINGS HE'LL HAVE TO LIVE WITH.

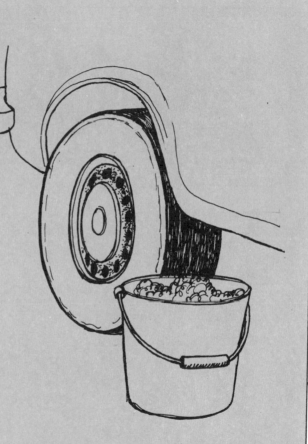

1

DAD, I'M NOT TOO HAPPY ABOUT CHANGING A WHEEL IF I GET A PUNCTURE. CAN YOU RUN THROUGH THE DRILL?

OK LOVE. WELL, FIRST PUT THE HAND-BRAKE ON AND, IF POSSIBLE, CHOCK ONE OF THE WHEELS. MAKE SURE THAT THE JACK IS ON FIRM GROUND, AND POSITION IT UNDER THE RIGHT PART OF THE CAR — CHECK WITH YOUR HANDBOOK. IF THE GROUND IS TOO SOFT, PUT A PIECE OF FLAT WOOD UNDER THE JACK.
USE THE LEVER IN THE TOOL-KIT TO PRISE OFF THE HUB CAP, OR USE A LONG SCREWDRIVER THEN, WITH THE WHEELBRACE, SLACKEN OFF ALL THE WHEEL NUTS ABOUT HALF A TURN. ACTUALLY, BOLTS ARE USED SOMETIMES INSTEAD.

CONTINUED:-

2

BUT SUPPOSE THE NUTS ARE TOO TIGHT FOR ME TO UNDO? I'LL BE IN TROUBLE THEN, WON'T I?

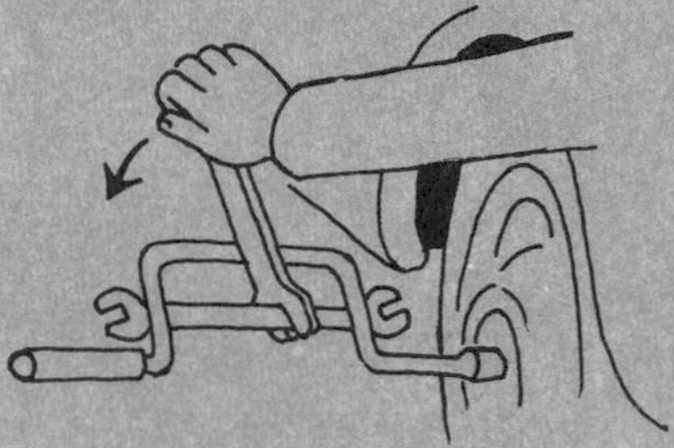

WELL IN THAT CASE, YOU CAN GET A BIT OF EXTRA LEVERAGE BY USING OTHER TOOLS, OR A LENGTH OF WOOD OR METAL TUBING. DON'T RE-TIGHTEN THE NUTS LIKE THIS, THOUGH.
NOW JACK UP THE CAR AND UNDO THE NUTS AND TAKE THE WHEEL OFF. FIT THE NEW WHEEL. IT'LL BE HEAVY, SO YOU MIGHT NEED TO USE A LEVER BETWEEN THE WHEEL AND THE ROAD TO HELP YOU LIFT IT INTO POSITION.

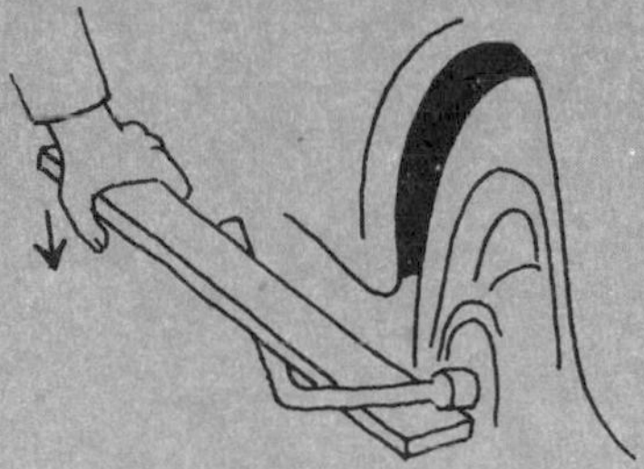

WHAT THEN?

WHEN THE SPARE WHEEL'S ON, RE-FIT THE NUTS WITH THE BEVELLED SIDE TOWARDS THE WHEEL. SCREW 'EM UP FINGER-TIGHT, LOWER THE JACK AND THEN TIGHTEN THE NUTS PROPERLY WITH THE WHEEL-BRACE, WORKING DIAGONALLY SO THAT THE WHEEL PULLS UP SQUARE. SNAP THE HUB CAP BACK ON AGAIN, AND YOU'RE IN BUSINESS.

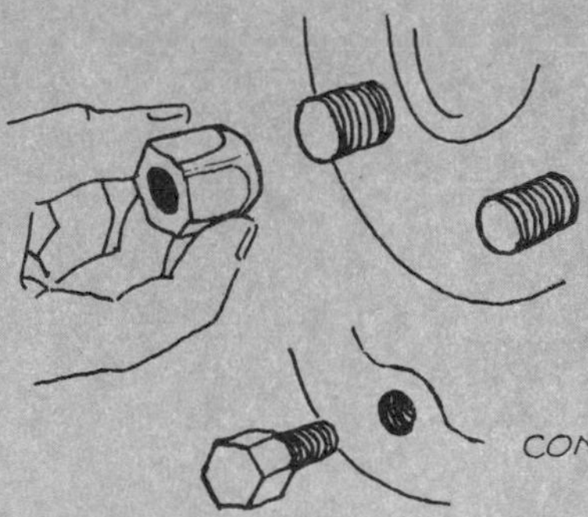

CONTINUED:-

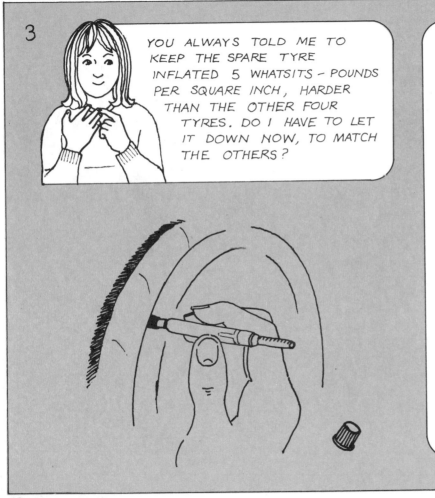

3

YOU ALWAYS TOLD ME TO KEEP THE SPARE TYRE INFLATED 5 WHATSITS – POUNDS PER SQUARE INCH, HARDER THAN THE OTHER FOUR TYRES. DO I HAVE TO LET IT DOWN NOW, TO MATCH THE OTHERS?

YEAH, A GOOD POINT, MARLE. CHECK WITH THE HANDBOOK TO SEE WHAT THE PRESSURE SHOULD BE, AND LET THE TYRE DOWN TO MATCH IT'S PARTNER, FRONT OR BACK.

USE YOUR PRESSURE GAUGE TO CHECK THE TYRES ONCE A WEEK AND DON'T FORGET TO SCREW THE LITTLE DUST CAP BACK ON THE VALVE AFTER – WARDS. WHILE YOU'RE AT IT, CHECK THE TREAD AND REMOVE ANY STONES OR FLINTS THAT ARE CAUGHT UP.

CONTINUED :–

4

ARE THEY THE CAUSE OF THAT REGULAR TICK-TICK NOISE I SOMETIMES HEAR WHEN I'M DRIVING ALONG? ITS QUITE LOUD AT TIMES, THEN IT GOES AWAY.

MMM, MOST LIKELY. SHARP STONES CAN CUT INTO THE TYRE IF YOU DON'T FLICK THEM OUT. USE A SLIM, BLUNT SCREWDRIVER, BUT MIND YOU DON'T DAMAGE THE TYRE. ALSO, HAVE A LOOK ROUND THE SIDE WALLS FOR CUTS AND BULGES, AND CLEAN OFF ANY OIL OR GREASE. IF YOU'VE GOT ANY DOUBTS ABOUT YOUR TYRES, LET ME LOOK AT 'EM. DRIVING ON DODGY TYRES IS NOT ONLY ILLEGAL — IT'S DAFT!

And so it went on and on, know what I mean? Gawd knows what our, or rather *my*, phone bills will be, thanks to all them transfer charge calls. Tell you what though, the Postmaster General will be laughing when he tots that little lot up. Earn himself an OBE I shouldn't wonder. And just look at that! Ever seen a carbuncular ear'ole before, have you? That's really painful that is. The others couldn't care less.

'Ah, poor Mr T,' says Janice with mock concern. 'Shall I put an hot thingy on it for you?'

'No you won't,' I says. 'Just you get on with filling in them MOT cerstificates.'

'You want to get yourself a telephone answering service Dad,' Geoffrey said.

'I am a flipping telephone answering service,' I says bitterly.

And Lionel's no help. He makes a hash of any phone messages he *does* take, getting names, addresses and what have you in a twist. He almost had me de-coking Group Captain wossisname's Capri the other day, when all it come in for was a tyre check. And talk about tactless! We've got a nice class of people round here – a bit top drawer some of them, so you have to watch yourself. Not Lionel. On one occasion a bloke rings up saying he had a flat battery.

'Tried pumping it up, have you?' says Mr Clever Dick. The bloke's livid, of course, and starts shouting and hollering for me. So I had to smooth things over diplomatically and get him sorted out. I give Lionel a right royal rollicking afterwards. Fat lot of good it does though. It just goes in one ear'ole and out the other – nothing to stop it, see? Vacuum-packed, his head is.

But, what made things worse was that Marle was always ringing me up when I was in the middle of something tricky or else up to me elbows in gunge. Not only that, time's money and I had a stack of jobs piling up and everybody was screaming for their motors. I knew this had to stop and I had been pondering on what I could do for some time.

All of a sudden it hit me – just like that.

'Eureka!' I shouts, waving a dipstick in the air, flicking oil all over the shop.

'You what?' frowned Lionel.

'No, Eureka!' I says, 'I've got it! How about if I write a book – well, perhaps a booklet. A simple guide to the motor car. Nothing complicated, just a run through some of the most important parts of the car. I could explain what to watch for, and describe how to do a few simple jobs.

With a bit of luck it might just keep Marle and Ron off me back – at least for a while'.

'Hardly your scene though Dad – writing, I mean,' retorts Lionel. 'Maybe not,' I says, 'but stone me, look who's talking. Your school reports was diabolical. Bottom of the class in English you was, time after time. All you was good for was spraying obscenities on the loo walls with an aerosol.'

'Even then he couldn't spell the PE mistress's name properly,' adds Geoff with a grin.

'Right,' I says. 'Anyway, I certainly know what's what as far as motors are concerned. As for the writing, I'll rough the book out first and then get Geoff to have a look through it. He'll help with the grammar and the spelling and that. You can type it out for me an' all, Janice,' I says. 'It'll make a change from cutting out them pictures of Starsky and Wossisname and pinning them round your desk.'

'I only do it 'cos this rotten desk hasn't got a modesty panel,' she snaps back. 'I was fed up with Lionel boggling at my legs.'

'Me boggle at your legs?' cries Lionel, his voice rising. 'You got to be joking. Blimey, they're like a couple of gnarled old tree . . .'

'All right, all right,' I chips in. 'Let's have a bit of hush, I'm thinking. Yeah, I can see it all now.'

'Well, you wouldn't if my desk had a modesty panel,' huffs Janice.

'Ssh, no I've got it,' I said 'Sidney Trimble's Guide to the Motor Car.'

'What about calling it POWER?' he says. 'You know, Petrol, Oil, Water, Electrics and Rubber?'

'Hmm, not bad Geoff, not bad,' I says. 'I like it.'

Anyway, cut a long story short, I got this little book done after a bit of a struggle, working nights and burning the midnight oil. Well, I had the incentive, see? Then I had a few copies run off at the local printers. I presented the first one, hot from the press, to Marlene and Ron (what I'd secretly dedicated it to, of course) with everything so firmly crossed that I nearly give meself a double hernia. Hang about, I think there are still one or two lying around somewhere. Yeah, look there under them tea mugs. That's it. You can have that one if you like – my compliments.

POWER

PETROL·OIL·WATER·ELECTRICS·RUBBER

Sidney Trimble's
Guide to the motor car

Before I get properly launched, let me give you a few words of warning about personal safety. All right, I know they're boring, but honestly I've seen quite a few workshop accidents in my time and believe me they're not a pretty sight. Most of them could have been avoided if people had taken a bit of care and not gone at things bull-at-a-gate. For instance:

Don't smoke or use a naked flame when you are working on anything connected with the fuel system or the battery. They both give off highly inflammable fumes.

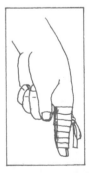

Don't let clothing, like a tie or a scarf, dangle in the engine compartment where it can get wound round the whirling fan or caught in the fan belt. The same applies to fingers – watch where you're poking them.

When you jack up the car, make sure that the jack is properly located and standing on firm, level ground so that it can't topple over.

Never crawl under the car when it's balanced on the jack. If you can't support the car on proper stands or ramps, forget it. Don't trust to housebricks – they can be killers.

Now I know you don't want to get involved in tricky dismantling jobs, but there are a few basic tools and bits and pieces that are always handy to have in the car. Even if you don't feel capable of tackling a job, someone with a bit of mechanical know-how might happen along when you're stranded and may be able to wield the appropriate spanner, or whatever, to good effect and save you calling the AA. Here's my selection – it looks a lot but the things won't take up too much space when they're packed away.

AA Members' Handbook
Car handbook
Jack
Wheelbrace
Sparking plug spanner and tommy bar
Tyre pressure gauge
Half-a-dozen open-ended spanners *(metric or AF depending on the make of your car – check with the handbook, local dealer or the AA)*
Small adjustable wrench
Pliers
Wallet of assorted screwdrivers
Spare fan belt
Temporary windscreen
Tow rope
Jump leads
Fire extinguisher
Torch or lamp
Insulating tape
Length of string and insulated wire
Aerosol of moisture repellent
Spare can of petrol
Sponge and chamois leather
Cleaning rags

Also keep a spare set of keys handy, and a lock de-icer for the winter (but not in the glove box!)

Many of these items are available from AA Service Centres.

Apart from the intricacies of the carburettor, which we won't go into here, the **PETROL** system is basically quite simple and doesn't need much attention.

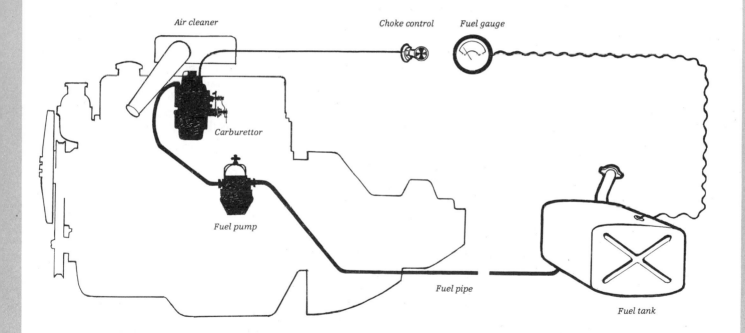

Air cleaner

Choke control

Fuel gauge

Carburettor

Fuel pump

Fuel pipe

Fuel tank

POWER

THE FUEL TANK AND GAUGE

The fuel gauge is operated electrically from a float in the tank – neither component needs any maintenance. If something goes wrong, you will have to get expert help to find the cause of the trouble and put it right.

Thousands of breakdowns a year are caused by drivers running out of fuel. One way of ensuring that you never get stranded with an empty tank is

to carry a spare can of petrol in the boot. But make sure that it's a proper metal container (never a plastic one) with a properly fitting, leak-proof cap like this one. Secure it safely, too.

The other way, of course, is never to allow the gauge to drop below $\frac{1}{4}$-full. This not only ensures that you won't run out, it also prevents the fuel system from becoming blocked. A petrol tank accumulates a certain amount of condensation, sediment and dirt. If you run with it almost dry, it's possible that these will get into the pipes and cause trouble.

The tank itself needs no maintenance, but occasionally check that the filler cap is sealing properly. If you should lose the cap (leaving it on a filling station pump perhaps) don't drive without it otherwise leaking fuel could cause a fire in an accident, or rain and dirt will contaminate the petrol and the engine won't run. If necessary, buy a temporary plastic one whittled down to fit the filler pipe until you can buy a proper replacement. In an emergency, push a wad of non-fraying rag into the top

of the hole. A locking petrol cap is a good idea, with petrol being the price it is today. You are unlikely to leave it behind too. Keys for the filler cap and the ignition will probably be on the same key-ring, so you won't be able to drive off until you have refitted and locked the cap.
In the unlikely event of your hearing a sucking noise when you remove the filler cap, it's almost certain that the tank's venting system is blocked. This should be seen to immediately because otherwise, at best, the engine will stop, at worst, the tank will collapse.

THE PETROL PUMP

Fuel is drawn from the tank and pumped to the carburettor by the pump which is either mechanical or electrical.

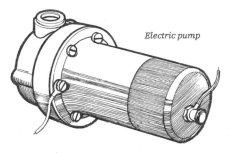

Electric pump

Electric pumps may be fitted in the boot, underneath the car or on the bulkhead immediately behind the engine; mechanical pumps are always fitted on the engine. Most cars nowadays have the mechanical sort, some of them topped by a glass bowl which makes it easy to see if it is full of petrol. All pumps have a filter which collects any dirt and sediment. If these build up, the filter and the fuel system will become blocked and stop the engine. This isn't very common, and anyway, a filter check is usually included in the car's regular servicing schedule. It's a simple job to clean the filter on most mechanical pumps, but electric pumps need more expertise and are best left to someone experienced.

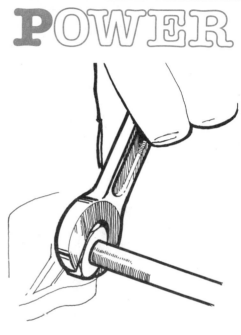

The fuel pipes from the tank to the pump, and from the pump to the carburettor shouldn't give any trouble, but their connections occasionally do. Petrol seepages can usually be cured by tightening the metal connectors with the appropriate spanner (taking care not to strip the thread in the soft metal of the pump and carburettor), or by tightening the clips on rubber connectors with a screwdriver.

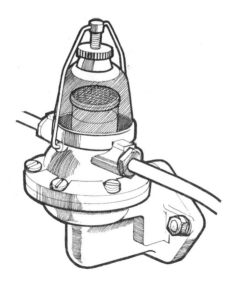

Mechanical pump

Flexible fuel pipes that are perished or cracked will, of course, have to be replaced. Fortunately, all the connections, except the one at the tank, can easily be seen and tightened without difficulty.

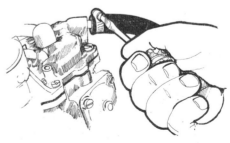

POWER

THE CARBURETTOR

The carburettor is quite a complicated instrument which has to mix the petrol with the correct amount of air to suit all running conditions. If it doesn't supply enough petrol the mixture will be weak, the engine will overheat and excessive wear will result. If it supplies too much, the mixture will be rich, the engine will sound and feel 'lumpy' and black smoke will come from the exhaust. Two types of carburettor are most commonly used:

The fixed-jet type and the variable-jet type.

Tuning the carburettor is a skilled job beyond the scope of the beginner, but it is very important. A badly adjusted carburettor wastes petrol, causes wear and creates pollution. Adjusting the carburettor, or more correctly the mixture and the idling (tickover) speed, forms part of all manufacturers' servicing schedules and some garages also offer a 'tune-up' of both petrol and ignition systems for quite a reasonable charge.

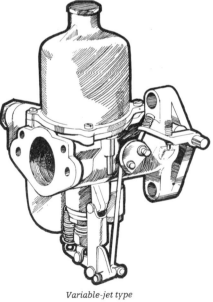

Fixed-jet type   *Variable-jet type*

THE AIR FILTER

It's essential that only clean air passes through the carburettor because dirt and dust will mess up the works and increase wear. For this reason, every carburettor is fitted with an air cleaner. This may be one of three types, but I'll simply mention here the most common one which is the paper-element type.

The element is made of resin-coated paper. As the air passes through the element it is cleaned. It's light, compact and easily renewed – usually every 12,000–18,000 miles in this country.

Some cars are fitted with air intakes that take cold or pre-heated air according to the engine's needs. Others have a do-it-yourself summer and winter setting and the filter case is usually appropriately marked; the handbook will say how. In the summer position, cold air is allowed straight into the carburettor. In the winter setting, the intake is turned close to the hot exhaust manifold so that the air is warm when it's sucked in. This prevents stalling and uneven running in the warm-up period and saves using too much choke.

POWER

THE CHOKE

When an engine is stone-cold, the petrol doesn't vaporise very well to form a good petrol/air mixture and a lot of it condenses and is turned back to liquid on the cold metal parts in the engine. To overcome this, the car is fitted with a choke which gives a very rich mixture for starting.

On some cars, the choke operates automatically with one press on the accelerator. After that you simply drive off and forget it; it cuts out according to the temperature of the engine. Most chokes, however, are controlled by the driver from a knob on the fascia marked CHOKE, C or, now more commonly, with this symbol.

POWER

To start a cold engine, the choke should be pulled right out (don't touch the accelerator) but as soon as the engine fires it should be pushed in as far as is necessary – usually about half-way – to keep the engine running smoothly. Drive off, then push the control home fully as soon as you can, otherwise you'll cause wear to the engine and waste fuel. Engines vary a lot in their need for the choke; you'll only find out how soon you can push it right home by experimenting. This may be after as little as half a mile but it will vary according to the weather, the engine obviously taking longer to warm up in winter.

PETROL GRADES AND STAR RATINGS

Choosing the right grade of petrol is very important because using a low grade will cause overheating and, possibly, detonation (better known as 'pinking'). This happens when the petrol ignites prematurely and raggedly, and it can cause serious engine damage. To help prevent this, certain additives – mainly lead – are put into the petrol.

Until 1967, oil companies caused a lot of confusion by giving their various grades of petrol fancy names such as Mixture, Regular, Premium, Super. But, as there was no agreement between the companies, the names didn't really help the motorist to choose the right petrol.

To make life easier, a star system was introduced that year, and motor manufacturers now state which star grade should be used. This is quite sufficient for most motorists. However, to please the enthusiast, they sometimes still quote the octane rating.

Drivers sometimes say to me that their cars seem to run better on one brand of petrol than another. This can be so. A three-star petrol, for example, could be 94, 95 or 96 octane. The difference isn't big enough to cause any problems provided the correct star rating is

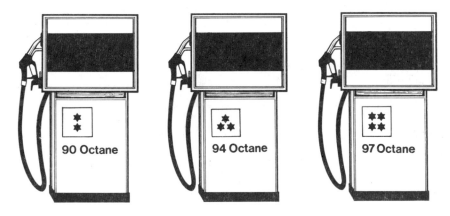

Minimum octane ratings shown

used, but an engine's taste for its petrol is like mine for my beer – it likes one brand a bit more than another.

If you've got a newish car, your handbook will probably tell you which star rating to use, or your local garage will advise you. If yours is an older model, the following list will probably help.

RECOMMENDED FUEL GRADES – PRE-1972 CARS

Star Grade	Make of car
	Austin/Morris
3	Mini (manual)
4	Mini (automatic)
3	Austin A40/Minor/1000
3	1100 (manual)
4	1100 (automatic)
4	A60/Oxford
	Citroen
3	Dyane
4	ID19, DS19, DS21

	Daf
2	33, 44
3	55
	Fiat
2	500, 600, 850
4	All others
	Ford
4	Anglia, Escort
4	Cortina, Capri
5	Twin Cam models
	Hillman
4	Imp, Avenger, Hunter Super, Minx
3	Minx III, V and VI
	Peugeot
4	404, 504
	Reliant
3	Rebel
	Renault
2	R4, R10
3	R6, R8, Dauphine
4	R8S, 1100, 16

POWER

	Triumph
3	Herald 1200
4	All others
	Vauxhall
4	Viva, Victor, Velox
	Volkswagen
3	1200, 1300 & 1500 single carb, 1600
4	1500 twin carb, 1600 TL

POWER

OIL is the life blood of any machine. Without it, working parts would soon wear out or seize up. Lubricate it, and it moves more easily and quietly. If you've ever ridden a rusty old bike or used a neglected lawn mower, you'll know what I mean.

When one piece of metal rubs against another, heat is generated and the faster it moves the greater the heat. The pistons in the average family car move up and down the cylinders at very high speed – nearly a mile a minute! Without oil the pistons and cylinders would be torn and scored before you could back out of the drive. Yet with proper lubrication an engine will run happily for at least 50,000 miles.

ENGINE LUBRICATION

You don't really need to understand the inner workings of the engine lubrication system, but this diagram shows just what a complicated route the oil has to travel in its work.

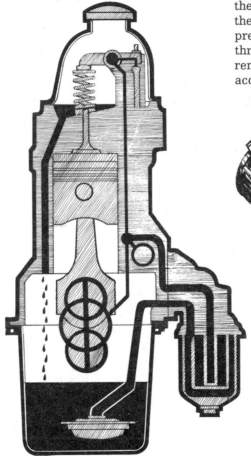

Oil is stored in the sump and when the engine turns, the oil pump pushes the oil round the engine under pressure. On the way, it passes through a very fine filter which removes the dirt that tends to accumulate in the sump.

The oil finds its way back to the sump simply by running down from all the pressurised parts, and in doing so, lubricates all the remaining parts which don't need to be lubricated under pressure.

Oil has a very hard life. It's churned and heated, diluted and contaminated, so it's no wonder that it needs replacing at regular intervals – 6,000 miles or six-monthly intervals is a reasonable maximum, but details are given in the car's handbook. It is very important to have the oil filter changed at the same time as the oil. There's no point in putting in clean oil if it is then going to be passed through all the sludge that has collected in the filter – it's like taking a bath in someone else's dirty water.

Every car is fitted with either an oil pressure gauge or a low-pressure

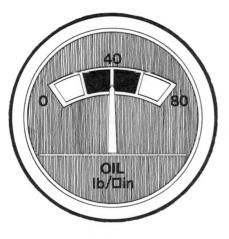

warning light (sometimes both) and it's important to use them.

If a pressure gauge is fitted, check what the correct reading should be in your handbook. The figure will usually be for a hot engine running at, say, 50mph. When the engine is started from cold the reading may be very high. Conversely, when the engine is idling hot the reading may be very low – this is quite normal. However, if the correct pressure, usually 35–40psi (pounds per square inch) does not register during normal driving, there is only one thing to do – STOP.

A reading noticeably lower than normal may indicate wear in the main bearings or the big-end bearings. Erratic variations in the reading or a fall from normal when cornering indicate that the level in the sump is low and that the oil is surging away from the point where it is picked up by the oil pump.

Most cars now have an oil pressure warning light, usually amber, which relieves the driver of the worry of varying oil pressure. Warning lights

POWER

come in all shapes and sizes so make sure that you can identify them on the fascia at a glance. When the ignition is switched on, the light will come on. Seconds after the engine has started it should go out and stay out all the time the engine is running. If it comes on while you are driving, the same advice applies (unless it occurs only at idling speed) – STOP and seek AA or garage help. Don't turn a blind eye and try to kid yourself that the gauge or the light is faulty; they rarely are. Many an engine has been wrecked by drivers failing to heed the warning.

THE DIPSTICK
All cars have a dipstick which is usually halfway down one side of the engine.

It's a simple means of checking the amount of oil in the sump and it should be checked every 500 miles or thereabouts.

POWER

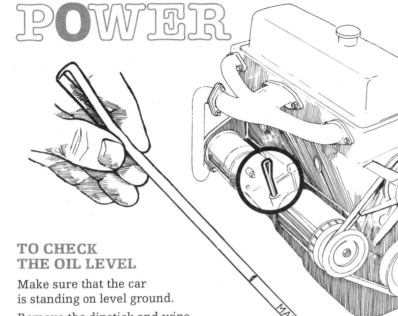

TO CHECK THE OIL LEVEL

Make sure that the car is standing on level ground.

Remove the dipstick and wipe it clean on non-fluffy cloth or kitchen paper.

Replace it in the cylinder block hole or guide tube.

Remove it again and look for the oil mark.

The oil level should always be between the minimum (low) and the maximum (high) marks. A litre (just under two pints) of oil usually represents the difference between the two marks.

If the level is below the minimum mark there will be insufficient lubrication and overheating will occur. This may well ruin the engine. If the level is above the maximum line excessive pressure will build up in the engine and cause leaks, or worse, serious damage – particularly to the clutch. Use a clean funnel when pouring in fresh oil and place rag round the filler hole to catch any spillage. Wipe up as necessary.

WHICH OIL TO USE

Oil companies work very closely with car manufacturers to produce oils to suit all kinds of engines and operating conditions. It's important, therefore, to use the correct type of oil recommended for your car. It's also preferable, though not absolutely essential, always to use the same brand.

Some car manufacturers recommend a single brand while others recommend a wide variety. Frankly, there's little or nothing to choose between the major brands so far as the ordinary motorist is concerned. The important thing is to use the correct type or grade of oil. In this country, fortunately, we rarely experience extremes of temperature and the majority of cars can use the same type of oil all the year round.

Most oils are graded by number and some have fancy names. It can all be pretty confusing, but any reputable garage will tell you if a named oil conforms to the car manufacturer's specification. If in doubt, stick to a 20W/50 grade of any well known brand and you won't go far wrong.

ADDITIVES

Modern motor oils are a very complex blend of ingredients and include a mixture of additives put in by the oil companies to give maximum performance with minimum wear.

All sorts of claims are made for other additives that you can buy and pour into your oil, but these are expensive and unnecessary if you use the type of oil recommended for your car.

These additives may or may not suit the oil you are using. If they do, no harm will be done, but there is seldom real evidence to show that they do any good. If they don't, they

POWER

may reduce the lubricating properties of the oil and cause serious problems.

Although the majority of car manufacturers don't actually ban the use of other additives, they don't recommend them. In fact, they often reserve their right to reject a warranty claim if engine failure results from their use.

Manufacturers *are* specific in their objections to the use of additives in gearboxes (especially automatics) however. They state categorically that they should not be used under any circumstances!

GENERAL LUBRICATION

I've been going on a bit about the engine because that's the item that needs the most frequent attention. All the other working parts are equally dependent on correct lubrication, however, although developments in recent years have progressively extended the intervals between services.

POWER

Although there are exceptions, most other parts need servicing at only 5,000 or 6,000-mile intervals, as recommended by the manufacturer. Some parts, which at one time needed oiling or greasing, are now pre-packed with lubricant and 'sealed for life' (whatever 'life' may mean!) and need no attention.

Components which *do* require attention must be dealt with at the correct intervals, otherwise premature wear and, possibly, failure will result. So it's important to keep a careful record of when your car is serviced and when the next service is due.

LEAKS

If leaks occur, regular topping-up to restore the correct oil levels is not the real answer. Leaks only get worse, never better, and they should be cured. A little drop of oil makes quite a mess and the start of leaks is easily seen by taking a quick look round the car once a week. One snag

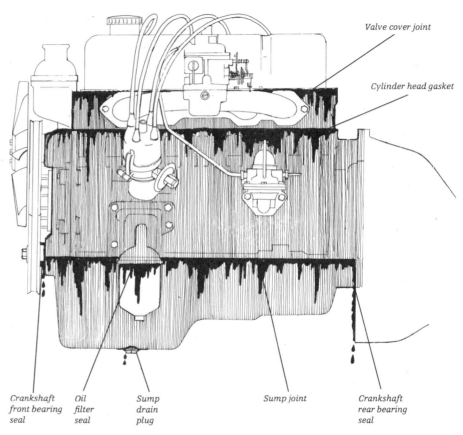

Valve cover joint

Cylinder head gasket

Crankshaft front bearing seal

Oil filter seal

Sump drain plug

Sump joint

Crankshaft rear bearing seal

Here are where most oil leaks or seepages occur.

is, though, that a small leak is often difficult to trace. A little oil goes a long way and it often spreads over a large area, either by being soaked up by dirt deposits, or by being blown back by the air-flow as the car moves along. A leak at the front of the engine, for example, could result in a mess at the back.

Most cars are prone to small leaks somewhere and one gets to know whether they are serious signs of trouble or simply inherent faults in design or assembly. In most cases, unimportant seepages, rather than leaks, may look messy but they don't result in oil actually dripping. If

you're in any doubt about a leak or a seepage – particularly at the wheels, which could mean faulty brakes – ask your garageman's advice.

There are, however, two valuable warning signs of real trouble. First, if frequent topping-up is necessary and, second, if oil actually drips on the ground when the car is parked. Either of these spells trouble so don't ignore them. This applies to all fluids used in cars – if they're disappearing or dripping, don't wait – do something.

POWER

BRAKE AND CLUTCH FLUIDS

All modern cars have hydraulic brakes and some also have hydraulic clutches.

Although it's not primarily a lubricant, hydraulic fluid does lubricate the moving parts in the brake and clutch systems. It's of such vital importance to safety, so far as brakes are concerned, that I must mention it here. If you know little or nothing about a motor car, NEVER interfere with the brakes and steering. If you do a botched up job on them they could be potentially lethal. Brakes and steering must be seen to by someone who knows what he's doing.

This doesn't apply to hydraulic fluid though. Modern cars have easily accessible fluid reservoirs so there is no excuse for failing to check the fluid levels regularly. A very slight drop in the fluid level is not uncommon, but if frequent topping-up is necessary, play safe and have a

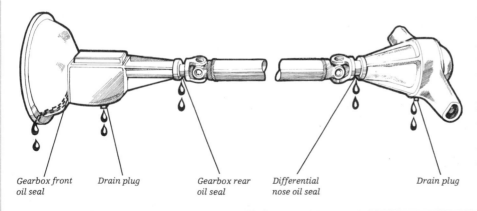

Gearbox front oil seal   Drain plug   Gearbox rear oil seal   Differential nose oil seal   Drain plug

POWER

thorough check for leakages carried out.

Most hydraulic fluids nowadays can be mixed quite safely but there are exceptions, so it's best to stick to one recommended by the car manufacturer. When you buy a can of fluid, buy a small one. Hydraulic oil is hygroscopic (it absorbs moisture in other words) and too much moisture can lead to a loss of braking efficiency. If a half-empty, large can is left about it will absorb quite a lot of moisture from the air, especially if the cap is loose. This is less likely with a small can. In any case, you shouldn't need much.

Even the fluid in the brake system will gradually absorb a certain amount of moisture and the brake people recommend a complete fluid change every 18 months, but that's certainly a job for an expert.

You may find it easier to use a small funnel for topping-up the reservoir(s). Wrap a cloth around the reservoir anyway to catch any spillage, because hydraulic fluid will attack and mark the paintwork in a flash. For this reason, throw the cloth away immediately you've finished the job. Top-up to within $\frac{1}{4}$in of the top of the reservoir, clean the reservoir cap and replace it.

There's no alternative to brake fluid, so never IN ANY CIRCUMSTANCES use anything else in the system. If you do, it could be as fatal as using red ink for a blood transfusion.

Tyred? Bald? Worn Out?
Consult the Experts.

Kenning Tyre Services stock all the leading brands and our own top quality Kenning Remoulds. We can supply most tyre sizes from our range of radials and crossplies - all at super value prices.
Why not call in and watch our Qualified Fitters in action? . . . Their advice could save you pounds - and your life!

KENNING *TYRE SERVICES*

KENNING

A complete Tyre Service throughout the U.K.

POWER

Mention **WATER** for a car and most people immediately think of the radiator. In fact, there are several essential uses for water in the running and maintenance of the car and for the comfort of its occupants.

THE COOLING SYSTEM

There are two methods of cooling a car engine – air cooling and water cooling.

Air cooling is restricted to small engines such as those used on most motor cycles and some cars like Volkswagen Beetles and the small Citroens and Fiats. Because a motor cycle engine is well exposed to air it needs no special installation, but most air-cooled car engines have a fan to force a draught of air over the engine. The engine design and installation have to ensure that good air-flow is possible otherwise the engine will quickly overheat. Apart from ensuring that the fan belt is correctly adjusted, the system needs no maintenance.

Air-cooling

Modern water-cooled systems incorporate a thermostat to give a quick warm-up, a pump to circulate the water more rapidly and a fan to draw, or blow, a faster flow of air through the radiator when the car is travelling slowly.

THE RADIATOR

The radiator is made up of a collection of very narrow tubes linked by wafer-thin strips of metal which are exposed to the air-flow. The surface area is made as large as possible. The greater the area cooled by the air, the more efficiently it works.

POWER

Old-fashioned radiators had relatively large diameter tubes, and it was quite common to seal small leaks temporarily by adding all sorts of odd concoctions to the water. These collected round the leak (if you were lucky) and blocked it. Modern radiator tubes are too narrow for such treatment and any attempt to resort to these old methods will clog the radiator, causing overheating and, possibly, considerable damage to the engine.

There are proprietary brands of anti-leak compound which can be used in an emergency, but there is only one real answer – a replacement radiator or a repair by a radiator specialist.

Most cars have a radiator cap which can be removed to top up the water, but take great care when removing it if the engine is hot. If you don't, there is a very good chance that boiling water will spurt out and badly burn your face and hands.

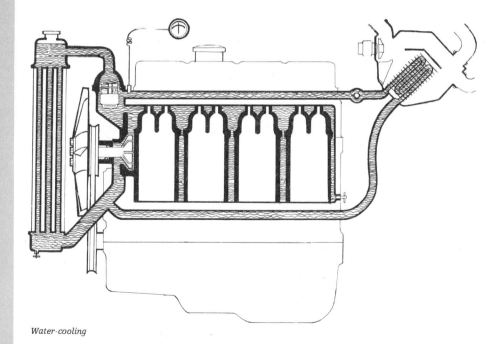

Water-cooling

POWER

You'll probably bang your head on the bonnet too, as you jump back in surprise.

Always wait at least a quarter of an hour before you attempt to remove the cap and, as an extra precaution, cover it with a thick cloth. When the cap is turned about half-way, you will hear a hissing noise as the pressure is released. Don't turn it any farther until the hissing stops – it's then safe to remove.

Radiators have an overflow pipe to allow excess coolant to drain off as it gets hot and expands. Many modern cars have a sealed system which should hardly ever need topping-up with coolant unless there are leaks. On these cars, the overflow pipe runs into a bottle which should be half full of water. As the water in the radiator gets hot and expands, the excess flows into the bottle. When the radiator cools and the water in it contracts, it sucks water back in from the bottle. Remember what I said before in the chapter on oil. If any fluid disappears and constant topping-up is necessary, find out why. If you don't, it may result in expensive repairs.

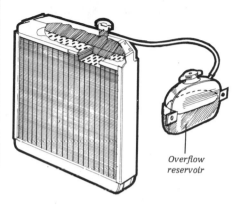

Overflow reservoir

ANTI-FREEZE

If you let the water in the cooling system freeze, it will have exactly the same drastic results as a freeze-up in a domestic water supply. To stop this happening, anti-freeze must be added to the water.

Most modern proprietary anti-freeze compounds are suitable for all types of engine, but others are suitable only for cast-iron engines and some only for aluminium. Quite a few engines these days have cast-iron cylinder blocks fitted with aluminium heads, so it is important to use the correct type, as stated in the car handbook. The book will also tell you how much to use. If you haven't got a handbook, use a universal proprietary brand of compound. A mixture of one part anti-freeze to two parts water will be safe for all winters in this country. You will probably need a 50/50 mixture in cold climates abroad though.

Don't wait until heavy frosts chill the air before adding anti-freeze. It costs a small fortune to replace a cracked cylinder block.
At one time it was necessary to drain off anti-freeze in the summer and put fresh in before cold weather set in, but this no longer applies. A good quality anti-freeze will last for two years and, because it contains anti-corrosive additives, it's best left in during the summer to stop rusting inside the system.

The strength of the anti-freeze will be reduced if the cooling system has been topped-up with water during the summer, don't forget, but a garage will check the strength for you with a special hydrometer. If any topping-up is needed during the winter, anti-freeze mixture must be used to prevent dilution and, possibly, freezing.

POWER

THE FAN AND WATER PUMP

The fan is nearly always mounted on a shaft from the water pump and the two are driven together by a V-shaped

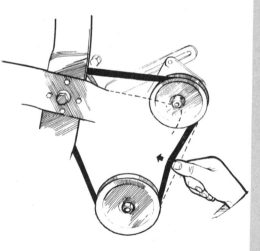

POWER

drive belt – the fan belt. This is driven from a pulley on the engine crankshaft. It's usual to drive the generator (dynamo or alternator) by the same belt, so it's essential to make sure that the belt is in good condition and that it's correctly adjusted to do its two-fold job.

Check the belt all round for splits, and have it renewed immediately if any faults are visible. Test the amount of slack by depressing it with your thumb on the longest run between the pulleys. Usually, $\frac{1}{2}$in–$\frac{3}{4}$in depression is allowable – any more and it's too slack, in which case the engine may overheat and the generator will not be able to charge the battery.
It's always a good idea to carry a spare fan belt for your car. The belt can easily be fitted at any time on the road without your having the trouble of locating a replacement.

Nowadays, increasing use is being made of electrically-operated cooling fans. They may be mounted in front of, or behind, the radiator and switch on and off automatically depending on the temperature of the coolant in the engine. When the engine starts to run hot, the fan switches on; when the engine has been sufficiently cooled, the fan switches off – it's as simple as that.
Many cars are over-cooled when on the move, and the fan could well be dispensed with. This, in effect, is what happens when you have an electric fan fitted, so don't worry if the fan rarely seems to work. It should only switch on in traffic or when the engine is idling.

If you are probing about under the bonnet with the engine running, don't be fooled by an innocent-looking, stationary electric fan. It could spring into life at any time and catch your fingers or wind round clothing.

THE THERMOSTAT

I won't go into technical details about the thermostat, except to explain that when the engine is cold it blocks off the outlet pipe from the top of the engine to the radiator and allows the engine to warm up quickly. Once the water in the engine reaches a predetermined temperature, a valve in the thermostat opens and allows water to flow through the radiator to be cooled.

If the engine takes an extra long time to warm up, it may be that the thermostat has jammed open. If it gets extra hot, the thermostat may be stuck in the closed position.

On some cars the thermostat is very difficult to remove, so it's not really advisable for beginners to tinker with it. There could be other causes of overheating which need expert diagnosis.

THE WATER TEMPERATURE GAUGE

If an engine overheats through a fault in the cooling system, it's likely that steam will be seen coming from under the bonnet. You will probably hear a bumping, bubbling noise and smell hot paint and oil. If the car is stopped straight away and allowed to cool, it is possible that no harm will be done, but the cause must be found before the engine is run again.

A lot of modern cars have a temperature gauge which is worked from a thermometer fitted in the cylinder head. Like all gauges and warning lights it's there to be used and any abnormal reading, high or low, should be investigated.

If the gauge reads lower than usual the thermostat could be faulty. ·If, in winter, it continues to show a low reading, the engine is probably being over-cooled and some form of radiator blanking may be needed. Seek advice before reducing the air flow, however, particularly if the car is fitted only with a temperature warning light.

If the gauge reads very high there could be many causes, all of them potentially serious, and the engine must be stopped. Similarly, if it reads very hot, then suddenly drops to cold, it is a sure sign that there is a serious loss of water which needs investigating straight away.

THE HEATER

The heater is actually a small radiator connected to the cooling system, and incorporates an arrangement of ducts operated by levers. These enable the driver to choose the temperature and direction of the air-flow (to the footwells or the windscreen, or both) while a variable-speed fan is provided to boost the air-flow throughout the car's interior at low speeds. Some cars, mainly Japanese, have a recirculatory position on the heater. This warms and re-cycles air within the car instead of drawing in fresh air from outside. It's useful in heavy traffic as it prevents exhaust fumes from being inhaled.

POWER

The most vulnerable parts of the system are the hoses which allow hot water to flow from the engine into the heater radiator (known technically as the matrix). All rubber eventually perishes, especially when it's subjected to hot water, so check the hoses regularly and have them replaced if they show signs of splitting, cracking or perishing.

POWER

If the heater never seems to warm up properly there is probably a fault in the engine's waterworks. It may be that the thermostat's sticking open or that there's an air lock in the system. Read the heating and ventilation section of your handbook carefully, and make sure that the various controls do what they say they are doing. Cold draughts when the controls say 'off' can usually be cured quite easily by having the cables re-set.

Some older cars' heater controls were not as efficient as they are today and a tap was fitted between the engine and the heater to allow the hot water to be turned off in warm weather.

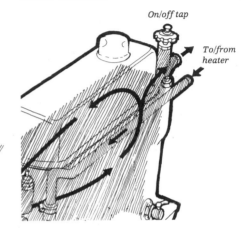

On/off tap

To/from heater

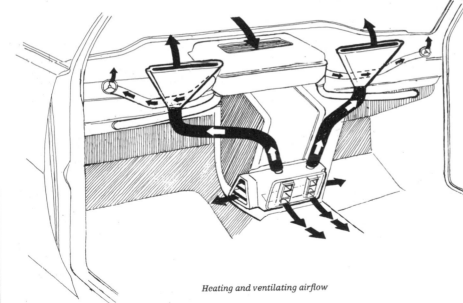

Heating and ventilating airflow

WINDSCREEN WASHERS

Windscreen wipers (see 'Rubber' section) can be effective only when the windscreen is wet. When there is only a little rain, or when muddy spray is thrown up by other vehicles, the wipers do more harm than good as they badly smear (and will probably scratch) the windscreen. To prevent this happening, windscreen washers are fitted and are a legal requirement on all cars

good either; nor does washing-up liquid, used for this purpose.

HEADLAMP WASHERS

Although they are still something of a rarity, headlamp washer jets are being fitted by an increasing number of manufacturers to provide full light output in dirty weather. They are usually fed from the same (enlarged) reservoir as the windscreen washers and are sometimes worked by the same pump. Some cars also have their headlamps fitted with wipers.

which don't have opening windscreens. They don't just have to be fitted either – they must be in full working order and the water container must be filled to make this possible.

The system consists of a water reservoir (washer bottle), a pump (which may be hand, foot or electrically-operated), supply pipes and jets to spray water on the screen. Marlene and Ron had a bit of trouble with theirs – have a look at page 18.

Plain water isn't much use for cleaning a windscreen, but add a measure of screenwash solvent to it

and traffic film and haze disappear quickly. Also add methylated spirit to the container in winter to prevent the fluid freezing. About a tablespoonful should do the trick. Never use engine anti-freeze for this purpose as it will cause 'rainbows'. Not only that, some anti-freeze mixtures are poisonous and could be dangerous if sprayed on the skin and eyes or if inhaled. They don't do the car's paintwork much

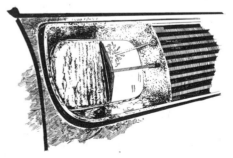

BODY CARE

Developments in paint technology have been very kind to the motorist in recent years. Old cars were 'painted' with cellulose which looked fine when the car was new, but it deteriorated fairly rapidly and regular polishing was essential.

Today, very hard paints are used and polishing is almost a thing of the past. A new car must never be polished for at least six months, to allow complete hardening of the paint, and will not normally need polishing to restore the shine more than once a year. Even that may not be necessary if the car is regularly and properly washed.

There's a right way to wash a car if the paintwork is not to be spoilt. No self-respecting housewife would start by washing her pots and pans and finish up with the glasses – she knows she would never have a clean glass. Similarly, the car owner must never wash the dirtiest part of the car first as abrasive dirt and grit will be spread all over the body and spoil the paint. The dirtiest part will be at the bottom where all the muddy spray hits the car. If it is very filthy it is a good idea to spray this gently first with a hose to help soften the muck, but do no more than that. Always start at the top, using plenty of cold or lukewarm water, and gradually work downwards. As you do this, the water will run down and float off some of the dirt at the bottom before you actually get down that far.

A proprietary shampoo, a little mild washing-up liquid or even a few teaspoonsful of paraffin in a bucket of water will help to remove stubborn traffic film, but never use household detergents or scouring powders. Keep rinsing your sponge to make sure that no grit is held in it, and change the water frequently to get rid of harmful dirt. Tar spots can be removed with a soft cloth dipped in white spirit or turpentine. Rinse well with plenty of clean water and dry off with a good quality chamois leather.

It's best to keep a separate leather for the windows because, no matter how careful you are, you may get a little grease, oil or polish on the one used for the car body. This won't harm the paint but will cause streaking on the windscreen.

If you prefer to use a hose instead of a bucket, never direct a powerful jet of water at the paintwork, particularly near the bottom, as it can cause grit to scratch the paint, and the water may well leak into the car. The best answer is to invest in a proper car brush which fits on the hose so that you brush and wash at the same time. The better brushes have an adaptor in the handle which holds a car shampoo.

The most serious effects of corrosion occur under the car body, especially after a bad winter when a lot of salt has been put on the roads. The salt mixes with mud and forms 'poultices' under the wings and other places where it is thrown up by the tyres. Hosing under the car is absolutely essential after a bad winter and should be done, in any case, once every couple of months throughout the year. Always do this before you wash the rest of the car or you will undo all your hard work.

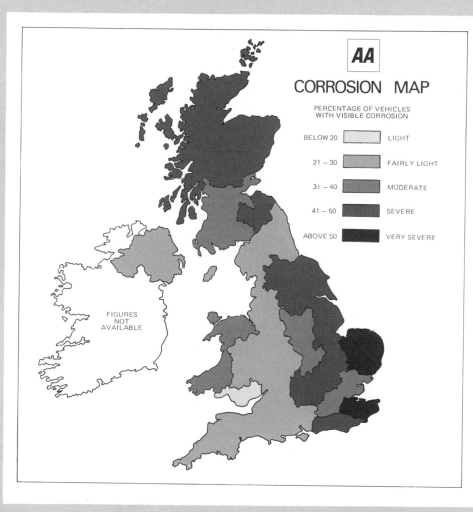

AA

CORROSION MAP

PERCENTAGE OF VEHICLES
WITH VISIBLE CORROSION

BELOW 20		LIGHT
21 – 30		FAIRLY LIGHT
31 – 40		MODERATE
41 – 50		SEVERE
ABOVE 50		VERY SEVERE

FIGURES
NOT
AVAILABLE

POWER

RAIN

Les Sims tells me that a few years ago the AA carried out a very detailed study of corrosion and its causes throughout the country.

It had previously been assumed that the worst conditions would be found in areas where there is a lot of industrial fall-out, or where a lot of road salt is used in winter.

Strangely enough though, the AA found that the level of corrosion in these areas is low compared with agricultural areas (due to pesticides, apparently) and warm areas where *less* road salt is used.

The reason for this is that the industrial areas have higher than average rainfall. Constant 'washing' of the underside of the cars by spray from the tyres and the washing away of harmful salts and chemicals down road drains keeps bodywork relatively free from accumulated mud and salt.

The answer's obvious – keep the underside of your car well washed with plenty of clean water.

POWER

The **ELECTRICAL** system is a very complicated arrangement of wires and accessories designed to provide the driver with a variety of services at the flick of a switch. It is expected to work under all sorts of conditions, hot or cold, wet or dry, day or night, yet it will rarely fail to do its job if it's properly maintained. Unfortunately the system is often neglected, with the result that almost half the breakdowns on our roads are due to electrical faults.

I reckon that electricians deliberately natter about diodes, capacitors, field windings, shunt resistors and hundreds of other fancy names just to show how brainy they are. In fact, you needn't worry about all the inner workings. All you really need to know are the names of the main components, what they look like and how to look after them.

THE BATTERY

The word battery means a number of things used or joined together, and in the case of the motor car it means a number of electric cells. Each cell is made up of a number of lead plates and is filled with diluted sulphuric acid (called the electrolyte). Practically all car batteries are 12-volt, but there are still some 6-volt types in use.

Some batteries have separate vent plugs, but more modern types have one cover, and sometimes two, for all the cells. When the cover is removed, you can usually see into the cells. The lead plates inside the battery come up to about $\frac{3}{4}$in from the top, and it is important to make sure that the level of the electrolyte is kept $\frac{1}{4}$in above the top of the plates.

As the battery is used, the level of the electrolyte will fall and will have to be topped-up. Fortunately, because of the chemical reaction inside, it doesn't have to be topped-up with sulphuric acid, but with pure water. This is either distilled or de-ionized water which can be bought from chemists, motor accessory shops or garages. Never use tap water. Some people use it without any ill-effects and in certain parts of the country you can get away with it. Generally though, tap water contains too many impurities which can damage the battery, even though they don't harm *you*.

Car electrical systems are either positive (+) or negative (–) earthed, and a battery has two terminal posts to which the main leads are connected. One lead (the earth) can clearly be seen to be attached to the body or the cylinder block, while

the other lead supplies the main feed to the electrical system.

One of the more common causes of electrical failure is dirty or loose connections of the leads to the battery terminals, but it only takes a few minutes to clean and tighten them, and to smear them lightly with petroleum jelly (Vaseline). See how Ron coped on page 14. Every part of the car's electrical system runs off the battery, so it's essential to look after it, but **please remember** these important warnings:

1 When a battery is charged it gives off explosive gases, so you must never use a naked light near the battery.

2 You can't get a shock from a car battery but you can get burned. So, don't wear rings or other metal jewellery when working on a battery. If the metal touches a battery terminal and another metal part at the same time it will cause a spark and may get hot enough to cause serious burns.

POWER

The same applies to the use of spanners or other tools. Great care must be taken to ensure that they don't bridge the battery terminal posts and cause a spark.

3 The battery is filled with acid. Any spillage must be wiped off immediately and the cloth you've used must be thrown in the dustbin before children get hold of it. It's also a good idea to wash the area with plenty of clean water.

Unfortunately, a battery can only hold a limited amount of current. It has to be constantly charged to keep it in good condition. This is done automatically by the dynamo or alternator, which, to make life easier I've been calling the generator.

If a car is used a lot for only short journeys the battery may suffer from under-charging. You can check the state of the battery's charge by measuring the strength of the

electrolyte with a hydrometer, the way I showed Ron on page 15.

THE GENERATOR

This is, as I say, either a dynamo or an alternator.

It is fitted to the side of the engine and is driven by the fan belt. If the belt isn't properly adjusted (see page 75) it will slip on the driving pulley and the battery will not receive the proper charge of

electricity. Three bolts (A, B and C) and an adjustable bracket hold the generator in place. When these are loosened the generator can be moved outwards to tighten the fan belt.

The output, or charge rate, of the generator is set by the manufacturer to make sure that when all the electrical components on the car are switched on, the generator will put back current being taken from the battery.

Dynamo

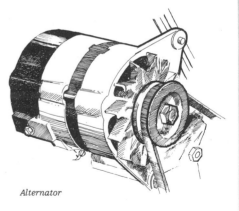

Alternator

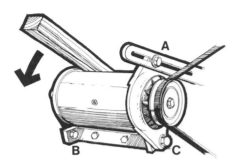

Some spare capacity is allowed for the fitting of extra lights and small extras, but if accessories, such as electric rear window heaters (which use a lot of current) are fitted, the generator may not be able to produce enough current to meet the demand of all the electrical components working at once. If this happens, the battery will run down, especially if you only do short stop-start runs. The answer is to avoid switching on too many things at once, or to give the battery an extra charge when the car is not in use.

BATTERY CHARGERS

If the battery goes flat or is run down you can give it a do-it-yourself boost with a home battery charger which is run off the mains electricity. These cost about £6–£12 and are easy to use. It's impossible to do any damage provided the right one is used properly.

As with any electrical appliance, it must be for the correct voltage which, in the case of the car, will be 6 or 12 volts but most chargers are suitable for either as they can be pre-set by a switch.

Here are the golden rules for using a battery charger:

A Make sure the battery is clean and topped-up with distilled water.

B Replace the battery vent plugs or cover after topping-up. Don't use the charger with them removed – modern batteries are liable to overflow without the plugs in place.

C If the battery is removed from the car, never charge it in a confined space; the concentration of gases increases the risk of an explosion

– they're unpleasantly smelly as well.

D If the car is fitted with an alternator, disconnect the main battery leads. Check which are the positive and negative terminals of the battery. The positive lead of the battery charger is normally red. Make sure that you connect positive to positive and negative to negative. Even a momentary mistake will cause a large spark and can damage the battery charger.

E Now switch on.

Most trickle chargers (as they are sometimes called) are fitted with an ammeter which shows the rate of charge. With a flat battery it will show an initial charge of about four amps (high charge), but after a few hours this will drop to about $1\frac{1}{2}$ amps (low charge) and remain at this level until the battery is fully recharged. This will usually take about 12 hours, so an overnight charge is quite enough. If the battery

POWER

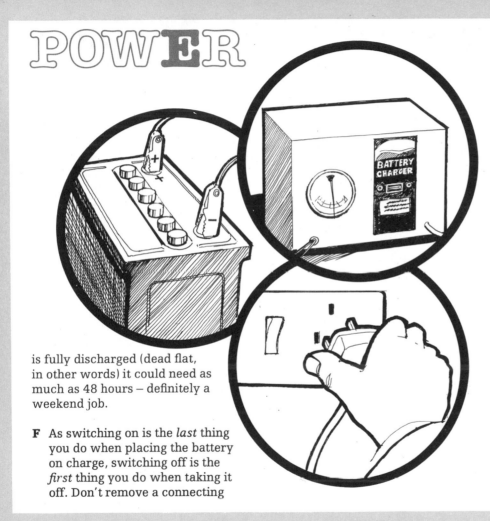

clip while the charger is on. It will cause a spark which could cause an explosion.

THE STARTER MOTOR

The starter looks very much like a dynamo but is fitted low down to the rear of the engine where it can engage with the flywheel and turn the engine.

The starter motor is a rugged piece of machinery which rarely goes wrong, despite the fact that it needs virtually no maintenance.

Like most mechanical parts it does sometimes fail (see Marlene's problem on page 16) but in most cases if it doesn't work it's the power supply rather than the starter itself which is at fault. Dirty or loose connections will cause failure, but the most common fault in the starter is worn pinion teeth. This calls for a new pinion assembly, but an exchange starter motor might be a cheaper solution.

The starter uses more electricity than any other component, and every time it is used it consumes as much current as a hundred headlamp bulbs. So it's not surprising that,

is fully discharged (dead flat, in other words) it could need as much as 48 hours – definitely a weekend job.

F As switching on is the *last* thing you do when placing the battery on charge, switching off is the *first* thing you do when taking it off. Don't remove a connecting

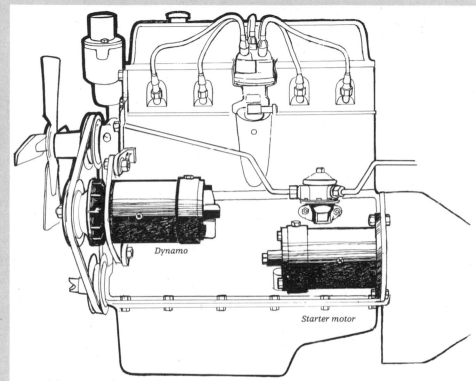

Dynamo

Starter motor

solenoid. This then makes a firm connection to the starter which can carry the heavy load.

At one time, all solenoids had a push-button which could be pushed to turn the engine for test purposes. A few still have a button, but it's not intended for regular use. As it has often been misused, some manufacturers no longer fit it.

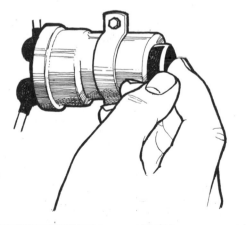

used for more than a minute or so, it will completely flatten your battery.

In fact, the starter motor uses so much current that if it was connected directly to the starter or ignition switch, very thick leads and big switches would be needed. For this reason it is fitted with its own heavy-duty switch, called a solenoid, on or near the starter itself.

When you press the starter or turn the ignition key all you do is to pass a small electrical current to the

POWER

INSTRUMENTS

If instruments and warning lights were not essential, manufacturers would not waste money fitting them. They're there to be used. If you ignore them you can hardly blame the car maker for any damage that results. Time and again I've investigated cases of serious failure, often resulting in bills for hundreds of pounds, where drivers have said that before it happened 'a little red (or amber) light came on', or the needle on an instrument dropped to zero, but they didn't think it was important, or didn't know what it meant.

Believe me, it *is* important and it's essential that you know what every instrument or warning light means. If you don't, make sure you find out or you could well fall out with your bank manager.

Often, only an ignition warning light is fitted in the fascia, but sometimes an ammeter or, more often, a voltmeter is provided.

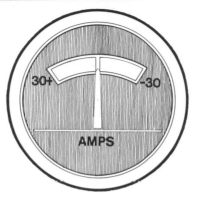

The ammeter

An ammeter reads like a set of scales. When it reads zero, the current being used is balanced by the amount that the generator is putting back into the battery. Under normal conditions, when the battery is fully charged, the ammeter should therefore read zero, or perhaps, record a small charge. This shows that the current being used is being made up by the generator. If it shows a perpetually higher charge or discharge, investigation is needed.

Immediately after starting, a higher charge will be shown as the generator puts back the current used. If too many components are switched on, a discharge may register. Neither reading is a cause for concern so long as it's only for a short time, but a zero reading should show within a few minutes. If it doesn't, seek advice. Faults could include short circuits, a defective generator and a broken fan belt.

The voltmeter

A voltmeter doesn't try to measure what the charging system is doing. It confines itself to the charge state of the battery. This should be between 13 and 15 volts for a 12-volt battery (odd though this may seem). Anything

less than 12 volts indicates that the battery is not being fully charged. Because the voltage levels needed can confuse the non-technical, many of these instruments have coloured bands instead of figures.

The ignition warning light
Although it's not actually an instrument, the ignition warning light is a valuable indicator as to whether the generator is charging the battery. It shines when an ammeter would be reading in the discharge zone, and goes out when the system is 'on charge'. The light is always red. It will naturally come on immediately the ignition is turned on, and go out as soon as the engine starts. If it comes on at any other time, beware. It may only mean that the fan belt is slipping but, whatever the cause, it should be investigated at once.

THE IGNITION SYSTEM
The ignition system is really a complete electrical system in itself. It's also the cause of more breakdowns than any other part of the car.

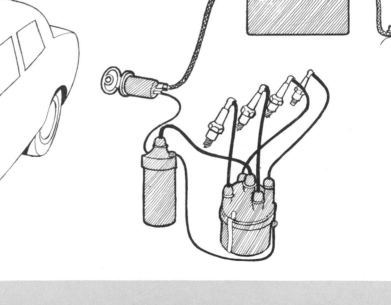

POWER

Regular maintenance is essential –
if you can't look after it yourself, you
must have it seen to by a garage.
Actually, it looks much more
difficult than it really is, and simple
attention will eliminate most of the
problems.

Wiring diagrams can be confusing,
but the simple drawing on the
previous page illustrates the
relationship between the various
components. So far as the beginner
is concerned there are only three
things to know about: the distributor,
the plugs and the plug leads.

THE DISTRIBUTOR

Although there are
several exceptions,
most distributors are
fitted in the side of the engine. A
distributor has a rotating centre
shaft with a cam lobe for each
cylinder of the engine. This cam
opens and closes the contact breaker
points as it rotates. Every time the
points open, a spark is produced at

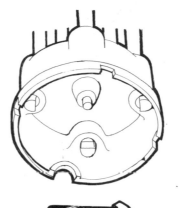

one of the sparking plugs. Every
6,000 miles these contact breaker
points should be cleaned or renewed.

Mounted on top of the cam is a rotor
arm which distributes (hence the
name) the high voltage current
through terminals in the distributor
cap to the sparking plugs via the
high tension leads.

Electric current is fed to the rotor
arm through a spring-loaded carbon
brush in the centre of the
distributor cap. The other main part
is the condenser (or capacitor). There
is nothing you can (or need) do to it,
so forget it. Note, though, that if the
ignition fails and the contact breaker
points appear to be badly burnt
prematurely, it is usually due to a
faulty condenser.

SPARKING PLUGS

The correct type of sparking plug
you should use is given in the car
handbook, and most garages have
charts showing which different
makes and types are suitable as
replacements.

Plugs are designed to work for at
least 10,000 miles, at which time it

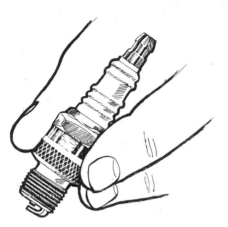

is sensible to have them renewed. This is usually done during a major scheduled service.

Halfway through their life (at an intermediate service, for example) plugs will need to be cleaned and adjusted to remove the build up of carbon and to restore the gap, where the spark is produced, to its original size. The gap increases due to the burning away of the points.

If this is done, plugs rarely give trouble unless the engine is worn and

burning oil, but they can play up if they get wet or dirty and the current runs down the outside of the plugs instead of jumping across the points. This is called 'tracking' and can be prevented by keeping the white, china-like tops of the plugs clean.

LEADS

It's important to ensure that all leads are free from cracks or splits, that they are kept clean, and that all their connections are tight. Although this is important for all electrical wiring, it applies particularly to the high-tension leads which carry as much as 20,000 volts. Incidentally, it is only these thick leads that can give you a shock when the engine is running. These, like the sparking plugs and other ignition components, are susceptible to moisture and should be kept dry as well as clean. If a hot car is parked in the cold, especially at night when the air is damp, condensation will occur. This is a major cause of ignition failure.

The problem is easily cured by using a 'damp start' spray. See how Marlene coped with damp electrics on page 12.

POWER

LIGHTS

All the lights normally fitted by car manufacturers: head, side, tail, number plate, stop (brake) and direction indicators are required by law. Not only must they be *fitted* but they must be maintained in working order. If you are stopped by the police on a brilliant summer's day and any one of your lights is not working you may be prosecuted. This might sound silly, but you never know when conditions may change, and a car with faulty lights is a menace to other drivers and to pedestrians.

I can't understand why British motorists are amongst the worst in the world for keeping their lights in proper working order and *for not using them.*

A car with only a nearside (left) headlamp working may easily be mistaken for a motorcycle. Faulty stop lights will fail to give following motorists a warning when you are braking. Inoperative direction

POWER

indicators won't show when you are about to turn, and badly adjusted lights may dazzle other drivers.

Very often it's much easier to see than to be seen, and in adverse conditions (and even in summer rain) a car with no lights or only side lights can't easily be picked out by other road users. It's a legal requirement to use dipped headlights in poor daylight conditions. I know that people's opinions of what is 'poor' will vary, but if there's any doubt, switch your lights on.

There's a stupid belief that having the lights on will flatten the battery. This is completely untrue provided the generator is working. As I explained, the generator puts back the current taken from the battery, so it's quite impossible for the battery to be run down by the lights unless it is overloaded by lots of use of the starter or by a lot of other things being switched on so that the generator can't keep up with the demand.

FUSES

The fuses in a car's electrical system are very similar to those used in household plugs and are very simple

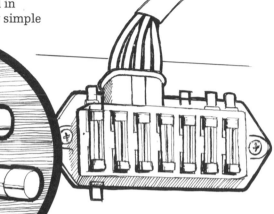

to replace. Some fuse boxes are well hidden, so make sure you know where yours is by checking in the handbook or by asking your garageman. Many a motorist has spent hours of misery waiting for help just for the sake of a fuse.

Having found where they are, check on the type and buy a few spares to keep in the car. If a fuse blows,

change it. If it blows again in a short time there is probably a serious fault which needs to be put right. Don't keep replacing fuses.

There's no substitute for the correct fuse, and using a higher amperage fuse or such things as nails, hair clips or silver paper will almost certainly guarantee a fire.

There are, of course, many other electrical components but few of them will cause you to be stranded if they fail.

LET GIRLING HELP YOU UNDERSTAND BRAKES AND SHOCK ABSORBERS

Brakes

Any intelligent motorist knows that a car's braking system needs regular attention. What he may not know is just what that attention should be. The free Girling brake chart tells you all about the system, and shows how with regular servicing and the right replacement parts your brakes can be kept in tip-top condition for maximum braking safety.

Write for your two free Girling Wall Charts, to Direct Mail Dept., Girling Ltd., 35 Boldmere Road, Sutton Coldfield, West Midlands, B73 5UX

Shock Absorbers

Very often these are little understood, yet they are also vital to safe car handling. Girling will send you a chart on shock absorbers. It shows the different types, the general function, and faults to watch for.

POWER

Apart from steel, **RUBBER** is the most essential material in a car. Accelerating, braking, cornering, or just plain motoring, your car depends on rubber.

TYRES

Tyres are the only contact between the car and the road, but few people realise that the actual area of contact is equal to the soles of two pairs of shoes. Imagine what would happen if two men tried to stop a car travelling at 60mph by putting their feet on the ground. Daft? Maybe, but the tyres have to do that and much more as well.

It's because tyres are so vitally important that special laws were introduced in 1968. The legal bit is rather heavy going, but I'll give you a run-down on the main points to watch for. Follow them and you'll stay safely within the law.

A Fit only those tyres recommended by the car manufacturer and stick

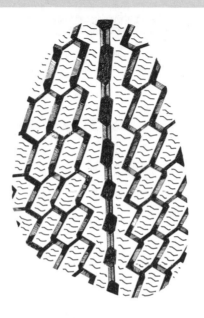

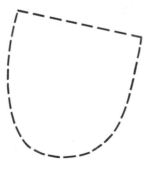

to one make and tread pattern. Whatever you do, don't mix cross-ply and radial-ply tyres as they've got completely different roadholding characteristics. Although it's permissible, but not advisable, to fit cross-ply tyres on the front and radial-ply on the rear, it's illegal, and downright dangerous, to fit them the other way round or to fit one cross-ply and one radial-ply tyre to the front or rear.

Radial-ply tyres are always marked Radial or R by law, but the cross-ply type aren't usually identified.

B Tyres should always be inflated to the pressure recommended by the manufacturer. They must never be under-inflated but over-inflation, up to about 6psi (pounds per square inch), is usually recommended for high speed motorway driving or when the car is heavily laden. The owner's handbook gives the recommended increases.
Incorrect pressures also cause rapid tyre wear.

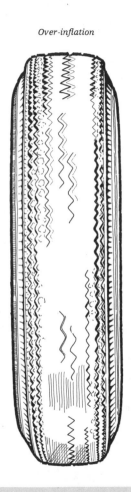

Over-inflation

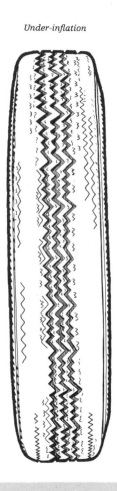

Under-inflation

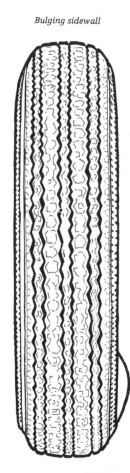

Bulging sidewall

C Any deep cut may be dangerous. If you see a cut, seek professional advice.

D Lumps or bulges are an indication that the outer rubber is separating from the main structure of the tyre. These can easily blow out and cause loss of control.

E Although a tyre may have the legal requirement of 1mm of tread depth for three-quarters of its breadth, it will still be illegal if even one small spot is so worn that the cords or fabric can be seen.

F One millimetre of tread depth over three-quarters of the breadth of the tyre is the legal minimum allowed, and the absolute minimum at that. Make a simple check with the rim of a coin. If the rim disappears into the tread grooves the tyre is probably within the law. However, anything less than 2mm of tread can be useless in an

POWER

involved in an accident through worn or damaged tyres your insurance cover may be invalidated. Play safe. Check your tyres regularly and if in doubt, seek expert advice.

Many modern cars are fitted with tubeless tyres. These are basically the same as tubed tyres except that they have an inner lining of soft rubber which makes them airtight. This replaces the conventional tube. Their greatest asset is that if they're punctured, they're much less likely to blow out. Opinions as to which is the best make and type of tyre to use vary enormously. My advice is

to fit whichever type the manufacturer recommends.

Remould or retreaded tyres are cheaper than new tyres and are quite satisfactory for general use, but they aren't suitable for continuous high speed driving.

If you're unlucky enough to have a puncture, the only answer is a permanent repair by vulcanisation. Tubeless tyres can have temporary repairs made by plugging from the outside with rubber plugs. The plugs must be red for easy identification and must not be used

emergency, especially on wet roads, and this should be regarded as the safe limit.

The fact that you're a beginner, or that you find the official jargon difficult to understand, is no excuse. YOU are responsible. Driving on faulty tyres may result in very heavy fines, endorsement of your licence or disqualification from driving. Furthermore, if you're

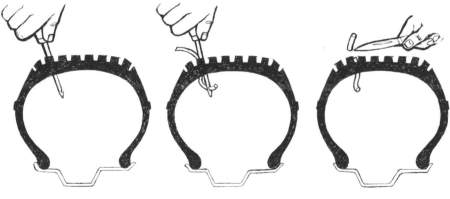

Inserting a tyre plug

for more than 100 miles at a maximum speed of 40mph.

At high speeds, tyres get hot and this increases their pressure. So much so that the plugs may blow out, causing deflation and loss of control.

The tyre laws don't apply to spare tyres while they are being carried, but they *do* apply immediately a spare tyre is brought into use. It is important, therefore, to ensure that the spare is in good condition and is correctly inflated at all times.

It used to be common practice to change the position of the wheels, including the spare, to even out the tyre wear. This isn't such a good idea any more because with modern suspension systems wheel balance has become more important. If the wheels are changed around, re-balancing will be necessary and fairly expensive. More important, however, is that tyres are now very expensive and if you wear out all five evenly you will have to replace them all at once instead of just two at a time.

HOSES

In the chapter on water, I explained that the radiator is connected to the engine and the heater by pipes. In practically every case these pipes are rubber hoses which are constantly under pressure and are subjected to frequent changes in temperature. Although the hoses are reinforced by cotton or nylon threads they still deteriorate with age and need careful attention.

Although nearly all brake pipes are metal, their ends are joined to the brakes by flexible rubber hoses; these allow the brakes to move up and down with the suspension and flex as the front wheels steer. Like other hoses, they will perish and, because they are attached to moving parts, may rub against metal parts and chafe. If there are any signs of cracking, leakage or chafing they should be replaced. All the working parts of the brake system also have rubber seals, but you can't see them. Nevertheless, if they perish they will leak. Remember the warning: if the brake fluid needs topping up frequently, find out why as soon as possible.

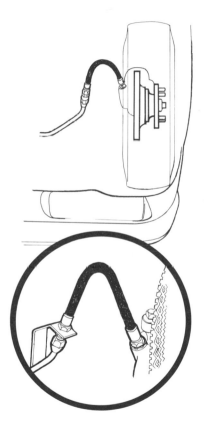

POWER

POWER

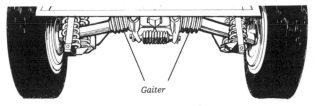

GAITERS AND BOOTS

No, nothing to do with footwear. Wherever working parts have to be protected against dirt and water getting in, or grease and oil getting out, they are fitted with rubber boots or gaiters. This applies particularly to the steering system of modern cars and the drive shafts of front-wheel-drive cars.

If these boots are allowed to split or to come loose, very expensive repairs will soon be necessary – apart from the dangers of failure which can cause accidents. It's impossible to tell you exactly where to find all the boots or gaiters as there are so many different designs, but they are usually easy to see and should be checked regularly.

Gaiter

Gaiter

WINDSCREEN WIPERS

Clear vision is one of the most important safety features and a lot of effort has been made by manufacturers to improve windscreen and window areas so as to provide as large an uninterrupted view out as possible.

Similarly, windscreen wipers have been developed to give the biggest sweep as is practicable. All this is a waste of time, however, if the rubber in the wiper blades is not looked after and renewed when necessary. When the windscreen is cleaned, the wipers should also be washed to remove dirt and grit which can scratch the glass. After about 12 months, the edges of the rubbers will probably be brittle and perished and will not clean the screen properly. Have them changed, or do-it-yourself, as soon as possible.

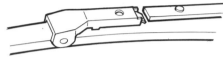

Replacement rubbers are cheaper than a whole blade assembly, and most garages and accessory shops sell them. It's important to quote the make and model of your car, or to take the old blade to the shop to make sure that you get the right replacement.

Lever back the locking clips at each end of the blade with a small screwdriver. Slide the rubber from the retaining clips.

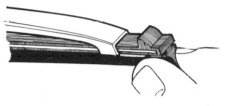

Insert the new rubber and lock it in place with the clips.

The blade should trail on both directions of its sweep – not trail one way and be pushed like a chisel the other. If the blade judders as it moves across the screen, remove the blade and twist the arm gently. Refit the blade and try again – on a wet windscreen. Keep adjusting the arm until the blade trails at the same angle as it travels in both directions. Most wiper blades are attached to the arm by a bayonet clip. Press the arm against the spring to disengage the peg and slide off the arm.

One sure way of cracking the rubbers, overheating the wiper motor and, very probably, scratching the windscreen is to leave the wipers working unnecessarily. As soon as it stops raining, switch off.

Well, that brings us to the end of the Rubber chapter and also to the end of my booklet. Hope it's been useful. But, just let me say again:
Don't interfere *with things you don't understand – especially the brakes and steering.*
Investigate *all losses of liquid – petrol, oil, water, brake fluid.*
Take notice *of all your instruments and warning lights.*
Read *and make sure you understand your car handbook.*
Finally, if in doubt, seek help from the AA or your garage.

It's a cruel world though innit? I mean you'd have thought that after all me efforts I'd have earnt meself a bit of peace and quiet wouldn't you? After all's said and done, I don't ask much from life. But no! Marle and Co was soon at it again. Mind you, there was a brief hiatus – is that the right word? Yeah, hiatus, in the phone calls. This was partly on account of me book and partly because they all shoots off to Frinton to stay with my sister, Dolly, for a week's holiday. (I gather she's making a slow recovery from the onslaught.) Quiet as the grave in here then, it was. The day after they gets back though it was business as usual, with the blower ringing its head off.

See, the thing was that me words of wisdom sort of whetted their appetites – made them keen to learn a bit more about what makes a motor tick. Now with Ron, a little knowledge is definitely a dangerous thing, and after reading me handy booklet he's not only got a string of genuine troubles with the car, but a spate of imaginary ones an' all – a bit like reading a medical dictionary when you've got an ingrowing toe-nail and thinking you've got a ruptured wossname.

Anyway, there I was just on the point of draining off a sumpful of filthy oil when the phone goes. Janice is down the caff getting the buns in, and Lionel's out on a breakdown, so Muggins has to answer it.
It's Ron.

1

ME AGAIN, LOVE!
MY LEFT LEG MUSCLE'S BEEN KILLING ME LATELY. THE CLUTCH PEDAL HAS GOT SO HEAVY TO WORK. RON'S MATE RECKONS THERE'S SOME— THING WRONG WITH THE CABLE.

YEAH, THERE VERY LIKELY IS, MARLE. ON YOUR MODEL THE CABLE RUNS CLOSE TO THE HOT EXHAUST, AND IT GETS DRY AND STIFF. I'VE TRIED LUBRICATING CABLES LIKE THAT, BUT I'VE NEVER HAD MUCH LUCK.
A NEW CABLE'S THE ANSWER. IT WON'T TAKE ME LONG TO FIT ONE.

WELL, COULD THAT BE THE REASON WHY THE ACCELERATOR'S A BIT JERKY TOO? I'VE BEEN FINDING IT'S BEEN MORE AND MORE TRICKY TO DRIVE THE CAR SMOOTHLY IN TRAFFIC LATELY. I'M LURCHING ABOUT ALL OVER THE PLACE.

CONTINUED :—

VERY LIKELY.

I'LL TRY LUBRICATING THE THROTTLE CABLE FOR YOU AT THE SAME TIME AS I LOOK AT THE CLUTCH. I'LL CHECK THROUGH THE LINKAGE AN' ALL – SOMETHING MIGHT BE DRY OR BINDING UP. BUT MOST LIKELY I'LL HAVE TO FIT YOU A NEW CABLE. IT'LL MAKE A WORLD OF DIFFERENCE IF THAT IS THE BOTHER.

THANKS, DAD. AND WHILE YOU'RE LOOKING AT THE CLUTCH CABLE, CAN YOU ADJUST THE CLUTCH ITSELF? IT DOESN'T ENGAGE UNTIL I LIFT MY FOOT NEARLY ALL THE WAY UP. I SOMETIMES WONDER IF I'M IN GEAR, THEN IT COMES IN AT THE LAST MINUTE.

YEAH, 'COURSE.

IF I FIT A NEW CABLE, I'LL AUTO– MATICALLY ADJUST THE CLUTCH. BUT IF THE CLUTCH LININGS ARE WORN, THERE AIN'T NO WAY I'M GOING TO BE ABLE TO GET THE PEDAL MOVE– MENT RIGHT!

CONTINUED :–

3

WELL, I WAS WONDERING ABOUT THAT.
SOMETIMES, LIKE ON A HILL, THE ENGINE SEEMS TO REV FASTER AS I ACCELERATE, BUT THE CAR DOESN'T GO ANY QUICKER. I THOUGHT IT WAS ME DOING SOMETHING WRONG. THERE'S A FUNNY SMELL SOMETIMES, TOO.

PROVIDED YOU'RE NOT RESTING YOUR FOOT ON THE PEDAL, 'RIDING' THE CLUTCH IN OTHER WORDS, IT PROBABLY IS WORN AND SLIPPING. IN THAT CASE, IT'LL MEAN A NEW CLUTCH. CHECK IT LIKE THIS: PUT THE HANDBRAKE ON, SELECT TOP GEAR AND GENTLY LET IN THE CLUTCH. THE ENGINE SHOULD STALL STRAIGHT AWAY. IF IT FADES OUT GRADUALLY, THE CLUTCH IS BADLY WORN.

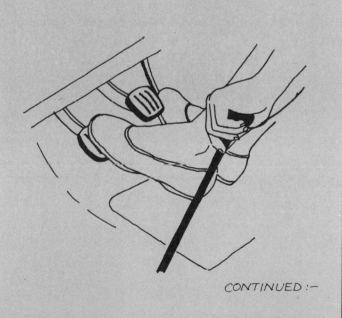

CONTINUED :—

4

The Clutch

COULD THAT BE THE CAUSE OF A METALLIC GRINDING NOISE THAT I GET WHEN I PRESS THE CLUTCH PEDAL?
A SORT OF DRY, SQUEALING SOUND?

BLIMEY, MARLE!
THE WHOLE LOT SOUNDS CLAPPED OUT! THAT'S YOUR CLUTCH RELEASE BEARING UP THE SPOUT. IT'S A WONDER YOU'RE STILL MOBILE! GET ROUND HERE SHARPISH.
I SHALL HAVE TO REPLACE THE WHOLE UNIT: CENTRE-PLATE, COVER AND RELEASE BEARING. IT'S NO GOOD DOING IT IN DRIBS AND DRABS.

CONTINUED :-

5

NOW LOOK HERE MARLE, DOING THIS CLUTCH IS GOING TO MEAN HAVING THE GEARBOX OUT. IF THERE'S ANYTHING ELSE WRONG, THAT YOU'VE BEEN HOLDING BACK FROM ME, FOR GOODNESS' SAKE LET'S HAVE IT. I AIN'T LUGGING THAT LUMP OUT AGAIN IN A HURRY!

WELL ACTUALLY, I WASN'T GOING TO TELL YOU YET BUT.... SEE, IT'S THE GEAR LEVER. IT GOES INTO THIRD OK, BUT WHEN I ACCELERATE, IT JUMPS OUT AGAIN INTO NEUTRAL. I HAVE TO HOLD IT IN THIRD, OR SKIP IT AND GO INTO TOP OR SECOND. OH, AND BY THE WAY, THEY MAKE A CLASHING NOISE IF I CHANGE GEAR TOO FAST. IS IT SERIOUS?

THUNK!

STONE ME MARLE, 'COURSE IT'S SERIOUS! FIRST OF ALL YOU'VE GOT GEAR WEAR, EXCESSIVE END-FLOAT OR A BROKEN DETENT. KNOWING MY LUCK, PROBABLY ALL THREE. AS WELL AS THAT, THE SYNCHROMESH HAS HAD IT, UNLESS THE CLUTCH IS DRAGGING. LET'S FACE IT, THE BOX NEEDS AN OVERHAUL. TELL YOU WHAT THOUGH, IT'LL SAVE YOU A BIT OF TIME AND MONEY IF I CAN GET AN EXCHANGE GEARBOX. I DON'T KNOW IF THEY DO 'EM FOR YOUR MODEL, BUT I'LL FIND OUT.

HELLO DAD. LISTEN, THE WIPERS SEEM TO BE THRASHING THEM-SELVES TO DEATH ON THE WINDSCREEN SURROUND. THEY'VE MARKED THE RUBBER TRIM AND I'M WORRIED THAT THE BLADES WILL BE DAMAGED. CAN I ADJUST THE WIPERS SOMEHOW TO STOP IT HAPPENING?

WELL, SEEING AS SNOWDROP'S IN THE AUTUMN OF HER YEARS, THE WIPER MECHANISM'S GOT A BIT WORN AND SLACK — THAT'S WHY THE BLADES ARE OVER-SWEEPING. YOU CAN RE-POSITION THE WIPERS TO PREVENT THIS HAPPENING THOUGH. CAREFULLY PRISE OFF THE OFFENDING ARM(S) FROM ITS SPINDLE WITH A COIN OR A SCREW-DRIVER, THEN REPLACE IT, MOVING IT A SPLINE OR TWO FURTHER ROUND FROM ITS ORIGINAL SETTING. TEST THE WIPERS ON A WET SCREEN. KEEP MOVING THE ARM ROUND A LITTLE AT A TIME ON THE SPLINES UNTIL THE BLADE CLEARS THE SURROUND AT THE SIDE AND BASE OF THE SCREEN. FINALLY, MAKE SURE THE WIPER RUBBER HASN'T BEEN DAMAGED.

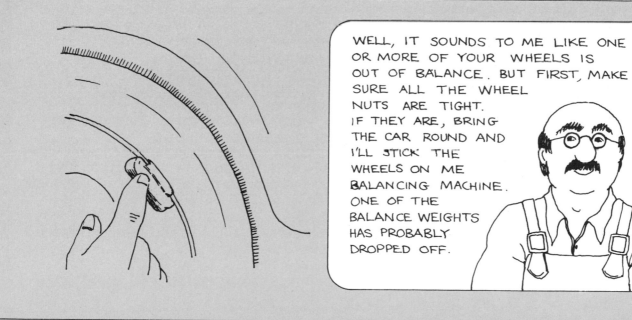

HEY, DAD, I'VE JUST COME DOWN THE BY-PASS, AND BLIMEY, WHEN I WAS DOING ABOUT 50, THE OLD STEERING WHEEL WAS WOBBLING ABOUT LIKE MAD — LIKE JELLY IN ME HANDS IT WAS. I SLOWED DOWN A BIT AND EVERYTHING SMOOTHED OUT. IT CAN'T BE WORN STEERING, YOU'VE ALREADY GIVEN THAT A GOOD GOING OVER. .WHAT'S CAUSING IT?

WELL, IT SOUNDS TO ME LIKE ONE OR MORE OF YOUR WHEELS IS OUT OF BALANCE. BUT FIRST, MAKE SURE ALL THE WHEEL NUTS ARE TIGHT. IF THEY ARE, BRING THE CAR ROUND AND I'LL STICK THE WHEELS ON ME BALANCING MACHINE. ONE OF THE BALANCE WEIGHTS HAS PROBABLY DROPPED OFF.

1

HAD A NASTY MOMENT YESTERDAY, DAD. RON NEARLY SHOT ME THROUGH THE WINDSCREEN WHEN HE HAD TO STOP SUDDENLY. I WAS WEARING MY SEAT BELT, BUT IT DIDN'T HALF HURT MY.... WELL, CHEST.
THAT CAN'T BE RIGHT, SURELY?

CERTAINLY NOT, LOVE. ACTUALLY, I'M GOING TO HAVE TO CHECK THE BELTS BEFORE SNOWDROP'S MOT BUT I RECKON YOU'RE NOT WEARING YOUR BELT PROPERLY.
LOOK, WHEN YOU PUT THE BELT ON, SEE THAT IT'S NOT TWISTED OR CAUGHT UP, AND MAKE SURE THAT THE DIAGONAL BELT (THE ONE ACROSS YOUR CHEST) FITS SNUGLY, LEAVING JUST ENOUGH ROOM TO SLIP THE FLAT OF YOUR HAND BEHIND IT, BUT REMEMBER THAT WHEN YOU TIGHTEN THE SHORT BELT THE BUCKLE SHOULD SIT TO THE SIDE OF YOUR HIP BONE (YOUR PELVIC WOSSNAME) NOT IN FRONT OF IT OR ACROSS YOUR TUMMY.
TELL YOU WHAT THOUGH, I'LL FIT YOU A NEW SET OF INERTIA-REEL BELTS. THEY TENSION THEMSELVES AUTOMATICALLY.

CONTINUED:−

2

MMM! WELL I SUPPOSE I DID HAVE IT A BIT SLACK, BUT I WEAR IT LIKE THAT BECAUSE OTHERWISE THE TOP BELT RUBS MY NECK AND MAKES IT SORE.

LET'S HAVE A LOOK-SEE. ON SOME CARS THEY GIVE YOU ALTERNATIVE, THREADED MOUNTING-HOLES FOR THE TOP ANCHORAGE, SO THAT THE SHOULDER BELT FITS COMFORTABLY. YOU CAN'T ALWAYS SEE THE OTHER HOLES BECAUSE THEY MAY BE HIDDEN BY THE TRIM, BUT YOU MIGHT BE ABLE TO FEEL 'EM.
IF THERE AREN'T ANY, I'LL GET ON TO THE FACTORY AND SEE IF THEY CAN SUGGEST A FITTING THAT'LL LOWER THE TOP BELT GUIDE. DON'T LET RON MESS ABOUT THOUGH, OR GO DRILLING ANY HOLES IN THE BODY. FITTING SEAT BELTS IS A SERIOUS BUSINESS, AND I'VE SEEN THE WAY HE BOTCHES ABOUT.

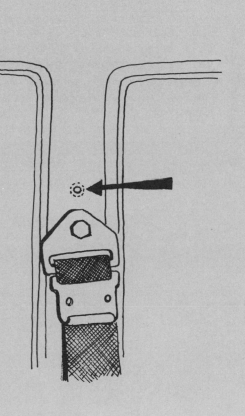

DAD, I'VE JUST HAD A PERISHING HOSE SPLIT AND I HAVEN'T GOT A SPARE. I MUST GET HOME SHARPISH, 'COS MARLE AND ME'S GOING SKITTLING UP THE KING'S HEAD AT HALF-SEVEN. ANY IDEAS?

SEEL A SPLIT

YEAH, WELL, IF THE SPLIT ISN'T TOO BIG, THE BEST THING TO DO IS TO WRAP SOME SPECIAL HOSE BANDAGE ROUND IT, BUT I DON'T SUPPOSE YOU'VE GOT ANY, HAVE YOU? NO, WELL IN THAT CASE, TRY WRAPPING A PLASTIC BAG ROUND IT, THEN BIND IT UP TIGHT WITH PLENTY OF INSULATING TAPE, FOLLOWED BY AN EXTRA BINDING OF STRING OR WIRE. YOU'LL HAVE TO TOP UP WITH WATER SOMEHOW. LET THE MOTOR COOL OFF FOR HALF AN HOUR OR SO BEFORE YOU DO THOUGH AND EVEN THEN, DO IT SLOWLY. BETTER TO BE LATE HOME THAN TO CRACK YOUR CYLINDER BLOCK. THEN YOU'LL HAVE TO SLACKEN YOUR RADIATOR CAP A BIT TO STOP THE SYSTEM FROM PRESSURIZING. DRIVE HOME STEADY, DON'T DO MORE THAN 30. I'LL GIVE MARLE A RING, TELL HER WHAT'S HAPPENED.

GUESS WHO? NO, LISTEN DAD, THE SPEEDOMETER'S PLAYING UP NOW. IT KEEPS MAKING A TICKING NOISE, AND THE NEEDLE WON'T STAY STEADY— IT WOBBLES FROM SIDE TO SIDE.
IT GETS ON YOUR WICK; HOW CAN I STOP IT?

IT SOUNDS LIKE A SPEEDO CABLE FAULT, RON.
IT'S EITHER DRY AND STICKING, OR OVER-OILY. ON THE OTHER HAND, THE CABLE COULD HAVE A KINK IN IT. EITHER WAY, I'LL HAVE TO HAVE A LOOK AT IT. IF I TAKE IT OFF, CLEAN UP THE INNER CABLE, LIGHTLY GREASE IT AND THEN RE-RUN THE WHOLE THING IN A SMOOTH CURVE, YOU SHOULDN'T HAVE ANY MORE BOTHER.

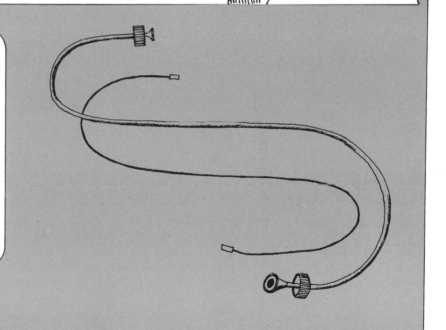

1

DAD, RON OILED THE HINGES YESTERDAY BECAUSE THEY WERE DRY AND SQUEAKY BUT THERE'S STILL A LOUD GRINDING NOISE WHEN I OPEN THE DOORS.
WHAT DO YOU THINK IT COULD BE?

IF RON OILED THE HINGES PROPERLY, ITS PROBABLY THE CHECK-LINKS THAT ARE SQUAWKING. THEY'RE USUALLY HALFWAY DOWN THE DOOR BETWEEN THE HINGES AND STOP THE DOOR FROM OPENING TOO FAR. GIVE 'EM A SPOT OF OIL OR A LIGHT SMEAR OF GREASE. DON'T OVERDO IT, THOUGH.

CONTINUED :—

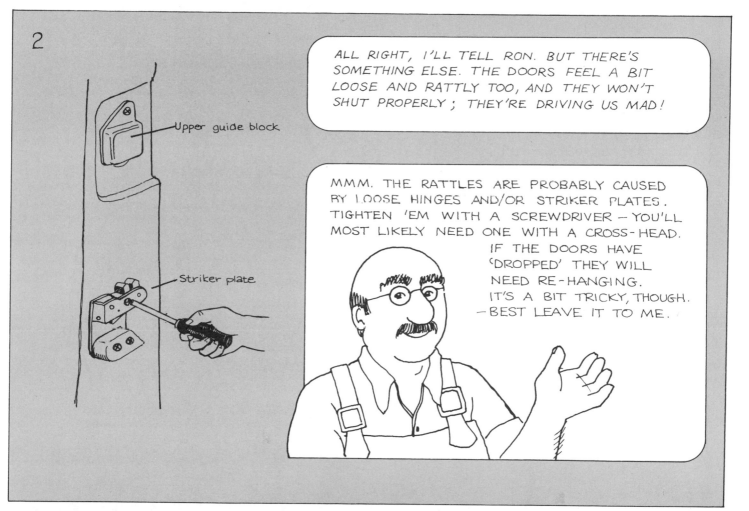

Drum Brakes

1

DAD, I HAD TO PUT THE BRAKES ON A BIT SHARPISH THIS MORNING AND THEY PULLED SO HARD TO THE LEFT I NEARLY WENT UP THE KERB. WHAT'S CAUSING THAT, THEN?

SOUNDS LIKE A SEIZED WHEEL-CYLINDER PISTON ON THE RIGHT-HAND SIDE. (THAT'S THE OFFSIDE), EITHER THAT, OR THE PISTON SEAL IS LEAKING AND BRAKE FLUID HAS GOT ON THE LININGS. WHICHEVER IT IS, IT COULD BE DANGEROUS. I SHALL HAVE TO HAVE A LOOK-SEE AND RENEW ALL THE SEALS WHILE I'M AT IT. IF THE LININGS ARE CONTAMINATED WITH FLUID I SHALL HAVE TO REPLACE THEM AN' ALL.

CONTINUED :-

2
TA DAD, YOU'RE A PAL. ACTUALLY I'VE BEEN GOING TO ASK YOU ABOUT THE ANCHORS, AND THIS HAS BROUGHT THINGS TO A HEAD. FOR SOME TIME NOW THE PEDAL'S BEEN GOING DOWN A LONG WAY TO THE FLOOR AND I'VE HAD TO PUMP IT TO GET A DECENT STOP – IT'S SORT OF SPONGY. I DON'T LIKE THE FEEL OF IT AT ALL.
BLIMEY, YOU DON'T ARF FLIRT WITH DANGER RON! THE BRAKES OBVIOUSLY NEED ADJUSTING – THE LININGS ARE WAFER-THIN I SHOULDN'T WONDER – AND THERE'S AIR IN THE SYSTEM WHICH SHOULD HAVE BEEN BLED OUT.. IT SHOULDN'T HAVE GOT IN IN THE FIRST PLACE. YOU SHOULD HAVE TOLD ME ALL THIS EARLIER – WHAT ARE YOU?

CAN YOU PUT MY MIND AT REST DAD?
I LIKE THE NEW INERTIA-REEL SEAT BELTS
YOU FITTED IN SNOWDROP, THEY'RE
EASY AND COMFORTABLE AND ALL THAT,
BUT I CAN'T HELP WONDERING IF THEY
WOULD REALLY LOCK UP PROPERLY IN
AN EMERGENCY. WHAT'S THE BEST WAY
TO TEST THEM?

15 MPH

EEEK

EEEK

MMM, I'VE HAD OTHER
PEOPLE ASK ME THAT.
THERE'S NO NEED TO WORRY
MY LOVE; WHEN IT COMES
TO THE CRUNCH, THEY'LL
WORK ALL RIGHT. YOU CAN
PROVE IT FOR YOURSELF,
THOUGH.
BELT UP, CHOOSE A QUIET
STRETCH OF STRAIGHT ROAD
AND WHEN THERE IS NO
OTHER TRAFFIC ABOUT,
ACCELERATE TO 15 MPH,
PUSH THE CLUTCH DOWN AND
THEN BRAKE HARD. THE
BELT SHOULD LOCK UP
INSTANTLY AND HOLD YOU
FIRMLY IN PLACE. IF FOR
SOME REASON IT DOESN'T
(WHICH I DOUBT), THERE IS
A FAULT WHICH NEEDS
SORTING OUT STRAIGHT
AWAY.

How to spot a real car duffer.

It's drivers who aren't members of the AA who are the real car duffers.

Even experts in motor maintenance realise the need for the security of AA membership.

So you can be sure that anyone who joins the AA and fixes the badge to the front of his car must have his head screwed on.

Our members know that the cost of a year's membership is a lot less than the cost of towing a broken-down car off a motorway.

And because the AA is on call 24 hours a day, 365 days a year, members are safe anywhere in the U.K.

But we offer much more than a free breakdown service.

Such as free advice on legal matters concerning the use or ownership of motor vehicles.

Routes and travel information for the UK are available free to all members.

We'll give free advice on a variety of insurance and technical matters and an inspection service for members purchasing vehicles.

And AA Relay, a valuable extension of the free breakdown service, gives an extra feeling of security to all Full Members.

If you break down and it's beyond prompt local repair, AA Relay will transport you, your car and up to four passengers to any destination on the mainland of England, Scotland and Wales.

So if you want to take advantage of services like these, or you think that a blown cylinder-head gasket sounds like a job for the plumber, join the AA now. Before it's too late–fill in the form overleaf and send it to us (no stamp needed.)

Please send details of AA membership to me at the following address:

NAME (Capitals) _____

ADDRESS _____

AA

Town _____

County _____

Post Code _____

CDG1

FIRST FOLD

Postage
will be
paid by
the Licensee

SECOND FOLD

Do not affix Postage Stamps if posted in
Great Britain, The Channel Islands, or Northern Ireland.

BUSINESS REPLY SERVICE
Licence No. BZ 501

2

The Automobile Association,
Membership Sales Development,
Fanum House,
BASINGSTOKE, Hants,
RG21 1BN.

THIRD FOLD AND TUCK IN

Please send details of AA membership to my friend(s) at the following address(es):

NAME (Capitals) _____   NAME (Capitals) _____

ADDRESS _____   ADDRESS _____

Town _____   Town _____

County _____   County _____

Post Code _____   Post Code _____

DAD, THE FLASHERS ON THE CAR HAVE SLOWED RIGHT DOWN TO A LAZY TICK JUST LATELY. HOW FAST SHOULD THEY FLASH AND CAN WE ADJUST THEM SOMEHOW?

LEGALLY, YOUR INDICATORS MUST FLASH BETWEEN 60 AND 120 TIMES A MINUTE AND YOU CAN'T ADJUST 'EM BECAUSE THEY'RE WORKED BY A SEALED AUTOMATIC SWITCH. THIS SWITCH (THE FLASHER UNIT) IS EITHER A SMALL CUBE OR A CYLINDRICAL CAN WHICH IS USUALLY FIXED UNDER THE FASCIA OR ON THE BULKHEAD UNDER THE BONNET. IT SOUNDS AS THOUGH YOUR FLASHER UNIT'S ON THE BLINK, BUT CHECK THE CONNECTIONS ON IT FIRST. IF IT'S STILL WORKING TOO SLOWLY, SIMPLY UNPLUG IT AND FIT A NEW ONE.

MR T, MARLENE WAS ON THE PHONE JUST NOW, ASKING WHAT SHE COULD DO ABOUT PAINTWORK CHIPS AND SCRATCHES. THEY'RE ONLY SMALL BUT SHE DOESN'T WANT 'EM TO GET ANY WORSE. I SAID YOU'D RING HER BACK.

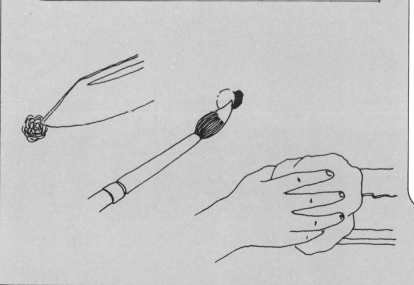

STREWTH! I CAN'T EVEN GO TO THE WOSSNAME IN PEACE. 'ELLO MARLE. PAINTWORK CHIPS, RIGHT? HERE'S WHAT TO DO. SCRAPE AWAY THE EDGES OF THE PAINT CHIP WITH A BLADE, THEN SMOOTH OFF THE EDGES AND RUB AWAY ANY RUST WITH A FINE EMERY CLOTH. NEXT, LIGHTLY TOUCH IN THE DAMAGED AREA WITH A FINE BRUSH USING A ZINC PRIMER. WHEN THIS HAS DRIED, FINISH OFF WITH THE RIGHT TYPE AND SHADE OF PAINT. WHERE PAINT IS SCRATCHED, CLEAN THE AREA WITH PETROL TO REMOVE POLISH OR GREASE. WASH IT WITH WATER, AND WHEN YOU'RE SURE THE AREA IS DRY, TOUCH THE SCRATCH IN WITH MATCHING PAINT.

1 I THOUGHT MY HEADLAMPS WERE SET PROPERLY, BUT OTHER DRIVERS KEEP FLASHING ME AT NIGHT. I SUPPOSE THE BEAMS MUST BE TOO HIGH. WHAT'S THE BEST WAY OF CHECKING THEM?

WELL THE BEST WAY RONALD, IS FOR ME TO DO IT ON ME BEAM-SETTER BUT YOU CAN MAKE A TEMPORARY ROUGH ADJUSTMENT YOURSELF. MAKE SURE THE CAR IS ON LEVEL GROUND AND CARRYING IT'S NORMAL LOAD, THEN DRIVE IT UP TO A WALL AND MAKE TWO MARKS ON THE WALL CORRESPONDING TO THE CENTRE OF EACH LAMP. NEXT, REVERSE 25 FT IN A STRAIGHT LINE AND THEN DRAW TWO CROSSES THROUGH THE CENTRE MARKINGS ON THE WALL.

CONTINUED :-

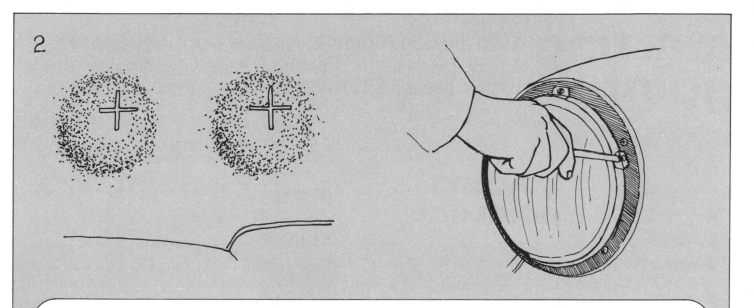

2

SWITCH ON THE LIGHTS (MAIN BEAM). THE TWO BRIGHTEST BLOBS OF
LIGHT SHOULD COME JUST BELOW THE CROSSES' HORIZONTAL LINES AND BE
AS CLOSE TO THE CENTRE AS POSSIBLE.
IF NECESSARY, ADJUST THE BEAMS AT THE SETTING SCREWS AT THE SIDE
AND TOP OF THE LAMP. (SOME CARS HAVE FINGER-SCREW ADJUSTERS AT
THE BACK OF THE LAMP, UNDER THE BONNET). WORK ON ONE LAMP AT A
TIME, WITH THE OTHER ONE COVERED OVER. QUITE SIMPLE!
LET ME CHECK 'EM PROPERLY THOUGH, AS SOON AS YOU CAN.

DAD, I'VE HEARD ONE OR TWO HORROR STORIES ABOUT AUTOMATIC CAR WASHES. DO YOU RECKON IT'S ALL RIGHT TO USE THEM – I MEAN, WHAT CAN GO WRONG?

WELL, SO LONG AS YOU USE YOUR LOAF THEY USUALLY DO A REASONABLE JOB. MAKE SURE ALL YOUR WINDOWS ARE CLOSED AND THAT THE RADIO AERIAL IS PUSHED RIGHT DOWN, AND SWITCH OFF THE WIPERS (AT THE IGNITION SWITCH) WHEN THEY ARE VERTICAL ON THE SCREEN. WING MIRRORS TEND TO GET KNOCKED ASKEW UNLESS THEY ARE TIGHT, AND WATCH OUT FOR ANY LOOSE TRIM WHICH COULD GET TORN OFF.
IF THE GARAGE DISPLAYS A DISCLAIMER SAYING THAT NO LIABILITY IS ACCEPTED FOR DAMAGE, LOSS OR INJURY CAUSED BY THE MACHINE, ANY CLAIM YOU MAKE PROBABLY WON'T WASH.

I HAD TO CALL INTO A FILLING STATION YESTERDAY BECAUSE I WAS LOW ON JUICE AND DIDN'T HAVE MY EMERGENCY CANFUL IN THE BOOT. I WANTED FOUR-STAR BUT THE PUMP HAD A PLASTIC 'NOT IN SERVICE' BAG ON IT. I DIDN'T WANT TO RISK USING THREE- OR FIVE-STAR IN CASE IT DID SOMETHING TO THE ENGINE. I ONLY JUST MADE IT TO THE NEXT GARAGE SELLING SNOWDROP'S GRADE. RON SAYS I WAS DAFT NOT TO USE THE FIVE-STAR PETROL. BUT I DIDN'T KNOW; IS HE RIGHT?.

NOT IN SERVICE

97 Octane

YES, FOR ONCE HE IS, MARLE! BUT YOU WERE RIGHT TOO, NOT TO USE THREE-STAR. SEE, THE THING IS THAT YOU CAN ALWAYS GO UP A GRADE (IT WON'T DO ANY HARM, EXCEPT TO YOUR FINANCES) BUT USING A LOWER GRADE THAN IS RECOMMENDED WILL CAUSE PINKING AND ENGINE DAMAGE.

ON THE WAY BACK FROM AUNTIE DOLL'S (SHE SENDS HER LOVE BY THE WAY), BOTH TRACEY AND TARK FELT QUEER. I DIDN'T FEEL NONE TOO GOOD MYSELF, NEITHER.
THE CAR KEPT SORT OF LURCHING AND BOUNCING ABOUT AT THE FRONT LIKE A BOAT IN A ROUGH SEA

IT'S YOUR DAMPERS LOVE — YOUR SHOCK-ABSORBERS — THEY'VE HAD IT.
AT LEAST, THAT'S WHAT IT SOUNDS LIKE.
GET RON TO GIVE SNOWDROP THE 'BOUNCE TEST'. STAND AT EACH WING TIP IN TURN, GIVE A HARD DOWNWARD SHOVE AND TAKE YOUR HANDS AWAY. THE CAR SHOULD BOUNCE UP AND DOWN ONCE, THEN STAY STEADY. IF IT BOUNCES AND TWITCHES MORE THAN ONCE THE DAMPERS ARE TIRED AND NEED REPLACING. YOURS SOUND PRETTY BAD, SO LET ME TAKE A LOOK AT 'EM AS SOON AS YOU CAN.
YOU COULD LOSE CONTROL OF THE CAR DRIVING AROUND LIKE THAT.

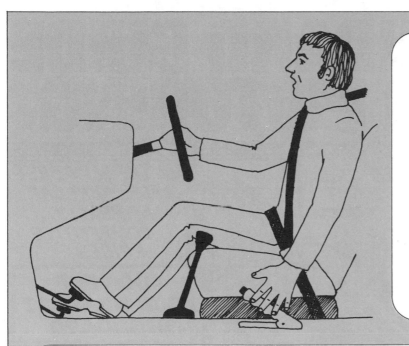

HEY DAD, A MOST AMAZING THING HAPPENED THIS MORNING. THERE I WAS, SLOWING DOWN AT SOME TRAFFIC LIGHTS, WHEN WALLOP! THE BRAKE PEDAL WENT STRAIGHT TO THE FLOOR. IT'S A GOOD JOB I GRABBED THE HANDBRAKE QUICK. I CARRIED ON ACROSS THE JUNCTION WHEN THE LIGHTS CHANGED, DROVE INTO A SIDE ROAD AND WHEN I TRIED THE BRAKE PEDAL AGAIN THERE WAS NOTHING WRONG. THE BRAKES ARE STILL OK NOW ; IT'S LIKE I WAS DREAMING IT BUT I SWEAR IT HAPPENED..
WHAT'S GOING ON ?

BLIMEY, IT'S A GOOD JOB YOU TOLD ME RON, AND DIDN'T DISMISS IT AS JUST 'ONE OF THEM THINGS'. YOU'VE OBVIOUSLY GOT AN INTERMITTENT BUT SERIOUS FAULT ON YOUR BRAKE MASTER CYLINDER. DON'T DRIVE THE CAR LIKE IT, IT COULD HAPPEN AGAIN AT ANY TIME. I'LL COME AND COLLECT THE CAR AND STRIP THE CYLINDER DOWN AND RENEW ITS INNARDS AS NECESSARY.

CAN YOU SETTLE AN INDUSTRIAL DISPUTE, DAD? THEY WERE ARGUING THE TOSS AT WORK THE OTHER DAY ABOUT WHETHER OR NOT IT'S A GOOD IDEA TO REV UP THE ENGINE BEFORE YOU SWITCH OFF. MY GUV'NOR RECKONS IT GIVES HIM EASIER STARTING IN THE MORNING. THIS OTHER BLOKE SAID HE WAS TOLD YOU SHOULDN'T DO IT, BUT HE DIDN'T REALLY KNOW WHY. WHAT'S YOUR OPINION?

VROOM!

MY OPINION IS RON, THAT YOUR GUV'NOR'S DOING HIS MOTOR NO GOOD AT ALL. THIS REVVING UP BUSINESS GIVES HIM EASIER STARTING BECAUSE NEAT PETROL HAS WASHED THE PROTECTIVE FILM OF OIL OFF THE CYLINDER BORES. BUT BECAUSE THE ENGINE HAS TO START UP 'DRY', HE'S CAUSING PISTON RING AND BORE WEAR. NOT ONLY THAT, THE PETROL IS DILUTING THE OIL IN THE SUMP, SO THE BEARINGS AREN'T BEING PROPERLY LUBRICATED. IT'S A BAD HABIT THAT HE OUGHT TO GIVE UP.

DAD, WHAT WORRIES ME ABOUT DRIVING VERY FAR IS THE FACT THAT I MIGHT HAVE A BREAKDOWN. CAN YOU RUN THROUGH WHAT I SHOULD DO IF I HAVE TROUBLE AND YOU'RE NOT ABOUT?

UNLESS YOU CONK OUT NEAR A GARAGE (SOME HOPES!) THE BEST THING IS TO LEAVE THE CAR IN A SAFE PLACE, PUT THAT RED WARNING TRIANGLE I GAVE YOU ABOUT 100 YARDS ALONG THE ROAD BEHIND THE CAR AND FIND A PHONE TO CALL FOR HELP. GIVE CLEAR DETAILS OF THE CAR, EXPLAIN WHAT'S HAPPENED AND GIVE YOUR LOCATION — SHOWN IN THE PHONE BOX. GO BACK TO THE CAR AND STAY WITH IT. THE AA WILL GIVE YOU FREE BREAKDOWN HELP AND A TOW TO A GARAGE, BUT MAKE SURE YOU ALWAYS CARRY YOUR MEMBERSHIP CARD WITH YOU — AND THE HANDBOOK.

IF YOU'RE IN TROUBLE ON A MOTORWAY, PULL WELL INTO THE LEFT ON THE HARD SHOULDER, SET UP YOUR TRIANGLE AND THEN TAKE A GANDER AT THE MARKER POSTS. THEY'RE PLACED EVERY 100 YARDS OR SO AND TELL YOU WHICH WAY THE NEAREST EMERGENCY PHONE BOX IS. WHEN YOU GET THERE, LIFT THE RECEIVER AND WAIT FOR THE MOTORWAY CONTROL TO ANSWER, THEN GIVE THEM THE GEN. GO BACK TO THE CAR, BUT DON'T GO WANDERING ABOUT ON THE HARD SHOULDER.

1

ER, THIS IS A BIT EMBARRASSING, DAD. I WAS SITTING SIDE-SADDLE, LETTING THE CAR ROLL DOWN OUR SLOPING DRIVEWAY, AND FORGOT TO LEAVE THE IGNITION KEY IN.
I TURNED THE WHEEL TO MISS TARK'S BIKE, THE STEERING LOCKED AND I MANGLED UP A COUPLE OF MARLE'S PLASTIC GNOMES; SHE'LL GO SPARE!
NOT ONLY THAT, I HIT THE DUSTBIN AND SMASHED ONE OF THE HEADLAMPS — I COULDN'T GRAB THE HANDBRAKE IN TIME.

BLIMEY, YOU SHOULD COUNT YOURSELF LUCKY, MY SON. YOU COULD HAVE HAD A REALLY NASTY ACCIDENT THERE. STILL, LEARNT YOUR LESSON NOW, HAVEN'T YOU?
NEVER MOVE THE CAR ABOUT UNLESS IT'S UNDER PROPER CONTROL, AND CERTAINLY DON'T TRY TO TOW IT WITHOUT THE IGNITION KEY BEING IN.

BRING HER ROUND AND I'LL FIT YOU A NEW HEADLAMP.

CONTINUED:-

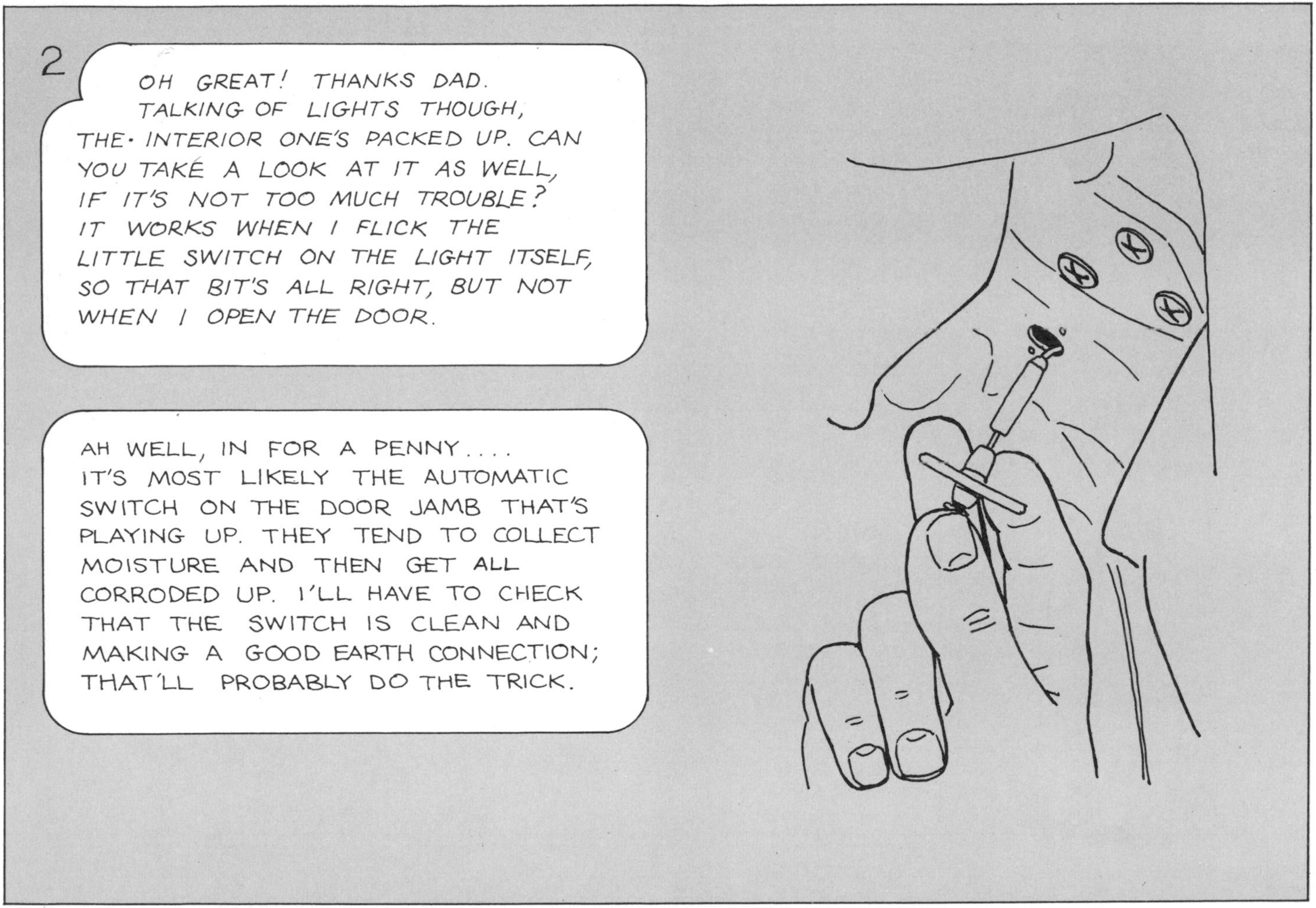
2
OH GREAT! THANKS DAD. TALKING OF LIGHTS THOUGH, THE INTERIOR ONE'S PACKED UP. CAN YOU TAKE A LOOK AT IT AS WELL, IF IT'S NOT TOO MUCH TROUBLE? IT WORKS WHEN I FLICK THE LITTLE SWITCH ON THE LIGHT ITSELF, SO THAT BIT'S ALL RIGHT, BUT NOT WHEN I OPEN THE DOOR.
AH WELL, IN FOR A PENNY.... IT'S MOST LIKELY THE AUTOMATIC SWITCH ON THE DOOR JAMB THAT'S PLAYING UP. THEY TEND TO COLLECT MOISTURE AND THEN GET ALL CORRODED UP. I'LL HAVE TO CHECK THAT THE SWITCH IS CLEAN AND MAKING A GOOD EARTH CONNECTION; THAT'LL PROBABLY DO THE TRICK.

Like a horror story innit? Only this one has a happy ending actually (I hope).

By subtly leaving the odd, new car brochure clipped under Snowdrop's windscreen wipers and draped over the steering wheel whenever the car was in here, and by praising the virtues of the latest small cars whenever I could discreetly work them into the conversation, Ron and Marle eventually come round to the idea of buying a much newer motor. The fact that I offered to lend them the money for it might have had something to do with it an' all. Anyway, they put down the deposit and are paying me off for the rest in monthly instalments. The next one's due two months ago.

It's nothing special, but it's a nice little runner, this 'Primrose'. Needs a new set of shock absorbers and that sort of thing, but it's a flaming sight better than that last contraption what should have been painlessly exterminated years ago. Honest, I feel as though a dirty great weight has been lifted off me shoulders. I'm actually getting down to working full time on *customers'* cars again, and for the first time in months, the . . .

Oh, my gawd, there goes the blower. I'll give you three guesses!

INDEX

Items in **bold type** are to be found in the cartoon sections.

INDEX

Items in **bold type** are to be found in the cartoon sections.